A Glimpse of Greatness: The Memoir of Irineo Esperancilla

*The work on this book occurred during the challenging days of the coronavirus pandemic and civil unrest across our country. I never expected to discover this glimpse of greatness in the midst of these trying times. Captivated by every hand-typed page of the original manuscript, I experienced not only the pride of my grandfather, but also the unwavering, quiet strength of my grandmother, and the unspoken strength of my mother, who was just a young girl at the time.

A GLIMPSE OF GREATNESS

THE MEMOIR OF IRINEO ESPERANCILLA

*A Glimpse into the Life of a Filipino American
Who Quietly Served His Family, His Country,
and Four Presidents of the United States*

COMPILED AND EDITED BY
MELINDA M. DART

ISBN: 978-0-578-37327-0
LCCN: 2022903043

Printed in the United States of America

This book is dedicated and written in loving memory and honor of:

The brave Filipinos who enlisted in the United States Navy in the 1900s; I salute your memory, your honor, and your sacrifices.

My grandfather, Irineo Esperancilla, whose remarkable character and dedication to duty allowed him to serve a unique role in the presidential history of the United States. Taking this glimpse into your life, I have learned more about my own life. I will always remember you as my Lolo, my Pop-Pop.

My grandmother, Maryann Esperancilla, whose beautiful life was an amazing inspiration to all who knew her. Her quiet strength and commitment as a military spouse enabled my grandfather to fully embrace his service to our country. Grandmom, this book is for you.

My beautiful mom, Ann Carreon Paje (Esperancilla), whose precious life was an example of true sacrifice and service to others. My dear dad, Juanito "Johnny" Paje, who was one of the brave Filipinos that answered his call to serve in the United States Navy, faithfully serving behind the scenes. Mom and Dad, you will always be my glimpse of greatness . . .

Acknowledgements

Special thanks to my family—my husband, Andre, whose unconditional love and support helped get this book published; my brothers, Nito and Joey, and my sister, Deb, who reflect this simple greatness every day; my wonderful and supportive 'Uncle Buzzy,' who carefully kept my grandparents' writings and gave them to me at just the right time; my children, Maria, Julian, and Anabelle, and niece and nephew, Jasmine and Jo, who will each carry the legacy of their great-grandfather and bring to the world their own glimpse of greatness. . . .

Preface

I must begin this book by saying every story, every detail, every recollection and reference would not have been possible, or even known, without the faithful efforts of my grandmother Mrs. Maryann Esperancilla. During my grandfather's military career, my grandmother knew what an important role he played in history. She longed for his story to be told. She kept every note, document, and artifact that pertained to my grandfather's life as a personal steward and ultimately Chief Steward of the United States Navy to four Presidents of the United States.

Note from Maryann Esperancilla

My devoted grandmother treasured these stories told and penned by her husband and documented his experiences with four of our nation's first families. She kept these written accounts safe long after my grandfather's death in 1976, and she continued to preserve this historical treasure throughout her life.

This book is the voice of the quiet greatness that often goes un-

Chief Esperancilla and Maryann Esperancilla
aboard USS Williamsburg

noticed. It is the amazing experience of a Filipino American and his comrades, and how they were destined to be that glimpse of greatness that was never and will never be recorded in the history books about four of the nation's Presidents.

Like many, I have often wondered why the Filipino navy recruits were assigned to presidential yachts and given duties as presidential stewards, among other important roles they played in the White House. Although many of their tasks may have been less desirable than others, I can only assume that these Filipinos' dedication and excellence in both character and performance were the reasons they were chosen to serve the United States in this way—simplicity in greatness. I also noted that my grandfather was always commended for his soft-spoken, unpretentious manner. These Filipino service members did not seek glory for themselves; they were honored to remain behind the scenes of the lives of the presidents they served.

Chapters one through six are written, compiled, and edited from the original typed manuscript of Irineo Esperancilla. This is the account of his personal observations, experiences, and memories serving in the United States Navy. In my grandfather's words:

I know that I did not have any part in history, but I was in the rare position to closely observe these four leaders of the greatest democracy in the world (not just as historical figures, but also as human beings). I feel, therefore, it is my duty toward the American people to put into writing my recollections of the great men whose service is the glory of my life, that of my children, my children's children, for the ages to come . . .

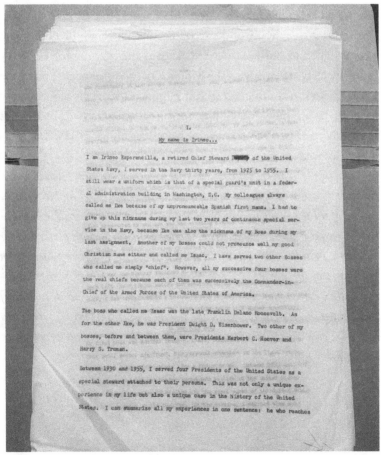

IE's original typed manuscript

Background

The United States Navy carries a long history of enlisting Filipinos, going back as far as 1901. An executive order signed that year by President William McKinley paved the way for young Filipino men to become a part of this branch of the US Armed Forces (Bureau of Naval Personnel, 2017). Many of these courageous natives of the Philippines were assigned to duties as stewards aboard the magnificent US Navy ships. In 1947, an article of the Military Bases Agreement allowed the United States to continue to recruit Filipino citizens for service in the navy. Up to two thousand Filipino recruits could join the United States Navy each year by 1954 (Bureau of Naval Personnel, 2017). The Military Bases Agreement ended in 1992.

During his career, Esperancilla has served Presidents Hoover, Roosevelt, Truman, and Eisenhower. For more than ten years he has been in charge of all the Navy stewards rendering service to the First Family. His service record is filled with letters of appreciation for services performed for the above Presidents, their families, and their many important guests from every part of the world. . . . His record of service, with its many indications of the satisfaction and pleasure of all whom he has served, is in itself sufficient indication of Esperancilla's capabilities. Esperancilla's retirement will be a great loss to the Navy and particularly to this unit in which he has served so well.

—Walter Slye, Lieutenant Commander, US Naval Reserve, 1955

CHAPTER 1

A Glimpse of My Life

My name is Irineo . . .

I am Irineo Esperancilla, a retired chief steward of the United States Navy. My colleagues always called me "Ike" because of my unpronounceable Filipino name. I had to give up this nickname during my last years of service in the navy, because "Ike" was also the nickname of my boss. I had another boss who could not pronounce my name and chose to call me "Isaac." I have served two others; one simply called me "Chief." The men I served were the real chiefs; they were Commanders in Chief of the United States Armed Forces. Between 1930 and 1955, I had the privilege to serve four presidents as a special steward attached to their persons. This was not only a unique experience in my life, but also a unique case in the history of the United States. From here, my story begins. . . .

એ

I was born in 1906, in the little village of Oton in the Philippines. Like many Filipinos, my dear father, Ciriaco Esperancilla, was a farmer. He wanted me to be a farmer with an education, so I was sent to a neighboring city called Iloilo, to study at the high school there. As a young high school student, I carried great pride for my country. I even dreamed of being the founder of an organization that brought hope and freedom to the Philippines. I remember writing in my high school notebook, "I only call those whose desire is burning for the freedom of his beloved Filipinas . . . long dreamed and buried in thy heart who love the Philippine Islands."

This loyalty to my beautiful homeland remained, but I was also fascinated by the open sea and the exalted history of the United States. Like many other Filipinos of my generation, I yearned to see America and what it had to offer me. As a young man, I felt something that is hard to describe—it was like a calling to serve America.

The extraordinary turn in my ordinary life occurred during the second year of my high school studies. My long-awaited opportunity came on Navy Day, December 1, 1925. The United States destroyer, USS *Noa*, appeared in the bay of Iloilo. This majestic ship undoubtedly carried hope and promise—something I had been longing for, both for my family and myself. Without hesitation or even informing my parents, I, along with other hopeful Filipinos, enlisted for four years in the United States Navy. There was no question in my mind that my future would be promising.

I was immediately assigned duty as a temporary steward. The *Noa* soon left the bay and returned to San Francisco, but I was transferred to a transport ship in Manila that took me all the way to Norfolk, Virginia. The dream of my young life became a reality.

My first few years in the United States Navy were typical enough for a navy recruit, but for me it was an exciting experience. With each opportunity I was given, I learned as much as I could and put forth my very best. I was first assigned as a personal attendant to an admiral aboard the light cruiser USS *Concord*. I received training and soon became accustomed to military life. From 1926 to 1929, this assignment took me to all the great ports from the Atlantic Ocean to the Pacific, including several ports of Latin American countries. I was truly honored and thankful to be a member of the Armed Forces of the United States of America.

I took my first long leave after serving for four years. I returned to my hometown in the Philippines to visit my parents and family. How I had longed to see them and to be back in my homeland. At the end of my stay, my beloved grandmother became very ill and passed away.

I couldn't bear the thought of leaving before her funeral, so I requested an extension to my leave through a wire telegram. I did not receive a reply. I was considered Absent Without Leave (AWOL) for two days and sixteen hours while I honored my grandmother at her burial. When I finally reported for duty, I was given thirty days of lost pay and forced residence in the brig. The official offense stated that I remained absent without the proper authority; I was devastated, to say the least, and believed my career might be over. You can imagine my sigh of relief when I was released after fifteen days for good behavior.

On August 8, 1930, I received orders to report for duty in Washington, DC. These orders did not make any special impression on me at the time; I was only excited at the thought of seeing the nation's capital. I reported for duty at the old Naval Receiving Station in Washington, DC. An officer ordered me to report immediately to a camp on the Rapidan River, near the Virginia mountains.

As a Filipino, even after serving five years in the US Navy, I had no idea what to expect at a place with such a strange name. Then I received the official word, which was beyond my every dream: I was assigned as one of the personal stewards to serve the president of the United States, Herbert Clark Hoover. From being AWOL in my little hometown of Oton in the Philippines to personally attending to the needs of the president of the United States, I knew God must have had a destiny for me.

CHAPTER 2

A Glimpse with President and Mrs. Hoover (1930–1932)

I am not a historian, only a modest witness to history; therefore, it is not my job to describe dates and accounts of historical events. My aim is only to contribute to history my personal observations. So, I continue my narrative. . . .

President Hoover was, in my eyes, the model of a fine gentleman. I spent my entire two years of service to President Hoover in the president's camp on the Rapidan in Madison County, Virginia, at twenty-five hundred feet elevation. This camp was an enchanting spot in the woods at the foot of the Blue Ridge Mountains. It's about one hundred miles west of Washington, DC. There were several wooden houses under the shadow of beautiful trees between the Mill Prong and the Laurel Prong. These were brooks that joined the Rapidan River near the camp.

Each house had a special name. The president and Mrs. Hoover's wooden house was called the *Brown House*. I remember a house called *Prime Minister,* named after its most famous guest, the prime minister of Great Britain. This house was reserved for important guests of the president. The "Town Hall" was a regular social gathering place for the hosts and guests of the camp. Meals were served in the "Dining Hall." There were several other wooden houses with picturesque names, such as "Five Tents," "Trail's End," "On the Hill," and the "Creel." Two adjoining camps on the other side of the Rapidan made up the marine camp and the camp reserved for visiting Cabinet members. The servants' quarters, as well as the house of the chief steward, were situated in the northern part of the camp near the Mill Prong. A presidential stable, named the "Hitching Rack," completed this beautiful presidential retreat.

Before the arrival of each presidential party, all of the grounds and houses of the camp were prepared, and a security routine was completed.

As I remember, the president and Mrs. Hoover spent almost every one of their weekends at Camp Rapidan during my service there. They frequently entertained guests; these included some members of the Cabinet, as well as a famous columnist and political writer. I even recall General Douglas MacArthur as one of the distinguished guests of the president at Camp Rapidan. I remember these two prominent leaders discussing the defense of the Philippine Islands, as Japan had a hold on Manchuria during that time. As a Filipino, that was especially significant to me.

の

At this summer residence, my boss woke up quite early. I brought President Hoover breakfast each morning around seven thirty. This consisted regularly of fresh orange juice, strong black coffee with sugar, eggs, bacon, and toast. While eating breakfast, the president intensely read the morning papers. He smoked his first cigar of the day after breakfast.

For lunch and dinner, very often my fellow stewards and I served roast chicken or lamb chops to the president, Mrs. Hoover, and the guests. As I recall these presidential meals, I picture the boss wearing a hat, a light blue coat, white trousers, and gleaming white shoes. He was a discreetly elegant gentleman.

അ

The president's wife was one of the most gracious first ladies I ever served. Mrs. Hoover was not only kind and caring to her guests, she was also wonderfully caring to those who served her—including the Filipino stewards, cooks, and me—who prepared the meals, maintained the rooms, and served in any capacity needed. Mrs. Hoover took command over us when the president stayed there.

The first lady loved flowers and liked to place healthy branches by the side of all the fireplaces and in the corners of the living rooms of each house. She wanted the room attendants to see that all the guests were supplied completely with all the comforts possible. We were ordered every day by Mrs. Hoover to place fresh boxes of fruit and candies in every room where guests stayed.

The first lady often planned and organized outdoor picnics. We frequently moved the tables under the shade of trees, sometimes three or four times before Mrs. Hoover decided on just the right spot. President Hoover usually attended these outdoor gatherings, but he was often quiet and seemed to always be in deep thought. He often left the table after he ate. In the case of bad weather, the gatherings were organized in the Town Hall. Mrs. Hoover presided over the events during this time.

After a presidential party stayed at the camp overnight, guests always complimented Mrs. Hoover on the outstanding service and delicious food. One day after lunch, the first lady led her guests on a tour around the camp, showing them unique parts of this presidential getaway. When Mrs. Hoover and her guests reached the kitchen unannounced, the (Filipino) pastry man was busy mixing the cake batter with his hands. The guests looked less than pleased; however, the gracious first lady looked at my friend with a smile and told him this was the only way to make a good cake! Mrs. Hoover assured her guests that the Filipino kitchen staff was excellent; the spotless kitchen and shining utensils definitely supported her statement. Mrs. Hoover complimented the cook on her way out.

On another occasion, Mrs. Hoover came into the kitchen while the Filipino cooks were making a native dish, *sotanghon*. Mrs. Hoover delighted in tasting the Filipino noodles; she even asked for more and ate a full serving.

ᏇᎧ

One day, when the president was in Washington, a group of Girl Scouts visited Camp Rapidan with their leaders. They were invited to dinner with Mrs. Hoover. She ordered us (the stewards and cooks) to prepare *eel* like a chicken dish. We did our best in preparing the eel as we were told. The guests believed chicken was on the menu and enjoyed their meal with the first lady. After dinner, she asked the Girl Scouts what they thought about the dinner. They answered unanimously that it was delicious. Mrs. Hoover enjoyed sharing with the girls that they had just eaten eel. Some guests looked puzzled, while a few of the Girl Scouts immediately became sick. The rest of the guests laughed along with their smiling hostess.

ᏇᎧ

I remember, one late rainy night, I heard the service bell ring for the Brown House. I jumped to my feet, and in no time, I was in the president's living room, where Mrs. Hoover was waiting for me. I knew something was wrong because I smelled smoke. When I flashed my light around the chimney, we discovered a crack. The first lady told me to go to the kitchen and bring back some flour. She made dough with the flour and some water, and together we patched up the cracked chimney. While we were working, she said, "Do you know when I learned this? When I was a girl scout . . ." Sure enough, the smoke was gone in a few minutes. The boss slept peacefully during the cracked chimney incident.

ᏇᎧ

During my time serving the Hoovers, I observed that the first lady seemed to be very conscientious of the needs of the community around her. One day, Mrs. Hoover walked around the camp with her guests and discovered there was a poorly equipped elementary school not far from the presidential summer residence. After organizing an action to help the school, the building was repaired and supplied with new equipment. From time to time, I recall the first lady inviting a school-teacher or other member of the modest surrounding community to lunch at Camp Rapidan.

℃

One recollection of Mrs. Hoover I will always hold in my heart occurred after my fellow stewards and I were authorized a short person-al leave to explore the Washington, DC area. Excited for a brief relief from our duties, we stopped at a roadside restaurant in Culpeper, Vir-ginia. My friend stepped inside the restaurant and went to find a seat. To his surprise, the waitress warned him, saying, "You cannot sit here!" At first, we thought something was wrong with those particular seats. We soon realized we were not welcome in the restaurant because of our Asian features. We left that restaurant and headed to Washington. The following week, we shared this incident with Mrs. Hoover. She immediately called the management of the restaurant. After her call, we never had any trouble in Culpeper or elsewhere. For Mrs. Hoover's outstanding support in taking a stand for Filipinos and others like us, I will always be grateful.

℃

During my service to President and Mrs. Hoover, I heard anoth-er story from a White House attendant that demonstrates the same support I experienced firsthand. The first lady organized a reception for the congressmen's wives. Before invitations were sent out, messages reached the White House that certain women would not attend if an African-American guest was attending. Mrs. Hoover did not allow this to intimidate her. She was not only a courageous first lady, but also a fine diplomat. Instead of one reception for all of the legislators' wives,

Mrs. Hoover arranged separate receptions so that all of the guests, regardless of their race, would feel welcome.

⁓

President Hoover liked to go horseback riding, hiking, and fishing at the camp. When he had good luck fishing, trout was often served to the guests on a first-come-first-served basis. I'm smiling as I remember watching the guests rush to the tables to eat the fish caught by the president of the United States.

One early morning, I think it was in 1931, the president put on his fishing outfit, took his fishing gear, and went out. I was on duty, and the president greeted me with his usual friendly "Good morning." The guests were asleep, and even the Secret Service men thought the boss was also still soundly sleeping. When they discovered the president was gone, they hurriedly came to me, and I pointed in the direction of the surrounding wooded area. Not long after that, the Secret Service men returned with the president. It was then that I understood that despite all its glory, it is very hard to be the president of the United States. In that moment, I saw the boss not as a historical figure, but as a human being. He simply wanted to enjoy some time fishing.

⁓

During the spring of 1931, I accompanied President Hoover on his official voyage to Puerto Rico and the Virgin Islands. I made the clothing preparations for the president to include six summer suits, twelve flannel trousers, one tuxedo, one silk hat, and six pairs of shoes. The presidential party's trip was aboard the USS *Arizona*. I was moved by the president studying to learn more about the history of the Virgin Islands, its people, and its relationship with the United States. The president and his party discussed the visit at length when we departed those islands.

ↁ

President Hoover was defeated by Mr. Franklin Delano Roosevelt in 1932.

During the final stay of the president and first lady at Camp Rapidan, they enjoyed themselves as usual with their guests. The president left early on Monday morning, while Mrs. Hoover and her guests departed later in the day. Before she left, Mrs. Hoover sent for all of the navy stewards. As we stood before the first lady, she began to thank us for the good and faithful services rendered to all who stayed at the camp. Then she told us they were leaving for California in a few weeks and, "If by chance any of you happen to see us, always speak first to us, for maybe because of our age we will not be able to recognize you at once." Mrs. Hoover shook hands with each of us for a final goodbye and left Camp Rapidan for good. I have never forgotten her kindness.

ↁ

That is a glimpse into my first experience as a presidential navy steward. On December 6, 1932, I received a commendation from the White House. It read that I was "commended by the president of the United States for cheerful and efficient services at the president's summer camp." This was a turning point in the history of the United States and in my career in the United States Navy. This was one of the rare and indirect coincidences between my private life and history.

CHAPTER 3

A Glimpse with President and Mrs. Roosevelt (My Best Years 1933–1945)

From the first day in his service, I was in awe of his superhuman strength of soul, which invigorated not only his own nation, but also everyone who had the privilege to work with him.

I was transferred from the presidential summer camp at Rapidan to the yacht USS *Sequoia*, which was anchored near the navy yard on the Anacostia River in Washington, DC. This magnificent ship was assigned as a presidential yacht as soon as Mr. Roosevelt was elected because the navy knew the new boss was a sea-loving gentleman.

Before President Roosevelt came aboard, my captain assigned me as his personal attendant. My specific order was to stay close to the president at all times and to be ready to assist him in everything at any given moment. This order meant that through the next twelve historic years, I would be standing by the president, sometimes up to eighteen hours a day, listening to him and watching him make decisions that would greatly impact our country and my life.

When my new boss first came aboard, with his famous and friendly smile, he called me and asked me what my name was. With great effort to check my strong Filipino accent, I stated, "Irineo Esperancilla, sir!" Right then and there, the president said he would never be able to pronounce my name. He asked if it would be alright if he just called me "Isaac." I had heard of and was amused by the many nicknames the president used for people, including "Pa" for a general, so I was quite satisfied with my new name. As Isaac, I served President Roosevelt on the USS *Sequoia* between 1933 and 1935; on the USS *Potomac* from 1936 to his death; in the White House; at Shangri-La; on the campaign train; on trips around the world; and very often at Hyde Park, his home above the Hudson River.

My specific orders aboard the USS *Potomac* stated:

1. Upon arrival of the president and until his departure, you will not leave the immediate vicinity of the president unless ordered to do so by him or an officer, or to go to the head, in which case you will return at once.

2. You will sleep on the fantail after all guests have turned in. In case of inclement weather, you may sleep in an easy chair in the wardroom. You will not go below at any time unless ordered to do so.

3. In case it is necessary to change uniform, you may obtain permission from the commanding officer at 09:00.

4. You will at all times be available in case of emergency to assist the president to his room and will close all windows in his cabin.

5. In case of abandon ship, you will also assist in transfer of the president to another ship or boat.

❧

I can easily recall a typical day in the White House with President Roosevelt. At six o'clock in the morning, I tiptoed into the president's bedroom and signaled Fala, his little dog, to come out. Fala spent most of the night near his sleeping master. The president's pet followed me obediently, and we went for a half-hour walk on the White House grounds or Lafayette Park. Sometimes, if Fala spotted a squirrel, I had to run after him, and this was quite a job. The Secret Service men often helped me. I would grumble at Fala when we finally caught him, and he seemed to understand. By six thirty, Fala slipped back into the president's bedroom. The little black Scotty usually spent the whole day with the president.

With the approval of Mrs. Casey, Pat and Irvin start their tour. On the way to the Capitol they greet Fala, the President's scottie strolling with an attendant near the White House.

CONTINUED ON NEXT PAGE   3

This photo appeared in Parade Magazine, The Washington Post, 1944

I entered the bedroom again at eight thirty and woke the president with a loud "Good Morning . . . I hope you had a good sleep, sir!" I brought the boss his toiletries, including a towel and comb. I held a mirror up for him to have a quick look. After that, he was ready for a glass of hot water with lemon juice as he glanced at the morning headlines. I served his breakfast at eight forty-five. Most mornings, the president would talk to Fala while eating and tell him to do tricks; then the president would give Fala a biscuit. (Fala always traveled with the boss on warships, yachts, planes, and even on the special presidential train.)

My morning job consisted of small tasks to ensure the president had every item he would need during the day. I cleaned his famous long cigarette holder, wound and set his watch, and filled his fountain pens with ink if needed. I also checked the president's medicines, eyeglasses, and his gold heart-shaped locket.

When the president finished his breakfast, I removed the tray and set up the wheelchair beside his bed. I helped him swing his legs to the side of the bed and move carefully from the bed to the wheelchair. The boss would then select a suit, tie, and a pair of shoes for the day. His first conference of the day often took place while he shaved and someone stopped by. After helping the president get dressed and stopping for a final check of his appearance in front of a large mirror, I wheeled him to the executive office. By then, he was also accompanied by aides, the press secretary, and the Secret Service.

During these wheelchair "trips," I learned a signal very early in the service of President Roosevelt. If people approached him as I was pushing the wheelchair and he did not want to continue the conversation, the boss would put pressure with his left hand on my hand. This signal meant that I needed to double my speed. I remember an early Cabinet meeting one day: We were in a hurry because the members of the Cabinet were waiting. As I pushed the president's wheelchair through the corridor, someone approached us attempting to engage the president in an important discussion. My boss gave me the signal, so I wheeled and walked faster. We arrived at our destination, and that person was not very happy with me. I felt bad because I could not tell him my reason for doubling my speed. This was a secret between the president of the United States and me, Irineo Esperancilla, Chief Steward of the United States Navy. After the meeting, I returned to wheel the president to his executive office.

I served the president his lunch around one o'clock in his office. If there were guests joining him, lunch was served in the dining room. Sometimes, the boss would take a short nap in the afternoon and then tackle the rest of his work until finished. Then, I'd help him if he went for an evening swim in the White House pool.

I handed Fala's dinner to my boss around six o'clock p.m., and he called his pet to come get dinner. The president watched, smiling, as Fala ate his food. Then there was usually a family gathering or cocktail time in the evening, followed by dinner around seven.

After dinner, I served coffee and liquor in another room. The president either prepared for a radio message, or there was a family movie. I was always welcome to watch the movie with the first family and guests or to be present during the radio broadcast. This was such a privilege for me to attend President Roosevelt's Fireside Chats. Sitting and listening in his presence, I always felt he was speaking to me as he spoke to the American people.

When he did not have an evening social engagement or a political conference, the president went back to his work, and I stayed until he went to bed. At this time, I would check so that things would be in order for the next day. I pressed his suits or shined his shoes in another room of the White House not far from my boss. Between eleven thirty and midnight, I massaged the president's legs while he read and then helped him get ready to go to sleep for the night.

"Good night, Mr. President. I will see you again in the morning, sir."

His usual reply: "Good night, Isaac. Please tell Mrs. Roosevelt to come in."

(During World War II, I stayed twenty-four hours a day in the White House. I observed President Roosevelt working late, as late as two or three o'clock in the morning. He was among the hardest working presidents I ever had the honor to serve.)

❧

I remember Hyde Park being a wonderful place of complete relaxation for President Roosevelt. In my recollection, he did not follow a particular schedule there and went to bed and woke up at any time. I still served his breakfast in bed and followed his morning routine, but it was much more laid-back. The boss took his time in the mornings, leisurely reading the newspapers.

When the weather was nice, President Roosevelt liked to use his special car, driving his guests and family members around the estate (followed by Secret Service men, of course). At this retreat, the boss also seemed to have the time to enjoy his stamp collection, listen to the radio, and just be with family.

ꙮ

I was with President Roosevelt when he visited South America in 1936. We made the long trip in the heavy cruiser USS *Indianapolis*. At the crossing of the equator, those who were crossing for the first time had to participate in the traditional ceremony of the "Pollywogs" and "Shellbacks." The president, who had crossed the equator before, was in a joyful mood, for it was also his second term as president of the United States. The Pollywogs, including me, endured being pushed into a tank of water. The ceremony concluded with the presentation of diplomas signed by the president himself.

We reached Buenos Aires a few days after the equator crossing. The historians reported the events of the 1936 Pan-American Conference of Buenos Aires under Roosevelt's presidency; I can only describe my personal impression. I shall never forget the indescribable popular enthusiasm that greeted the president in each of the South American countries we stopped. I can still hear the thunderous shouting of the crowds, "Viva, Viva, Viva el Presidente Roosevelt." In Buenos Aires alone, the number of people that gathered to see him was estimated at over two hundred and fifty thousand. I was standing behind the boss as he waved toward the crowd saying, "I love it, I love it. . . ."

ꙮ

I was again with the president on his vacation in the Pacific and his visit to the Galapagos Islands in 1938. I remember the boss always seemed to have good luck fishing on trips; he caught a huge marlin on this trip. When we returned to the ship after fishing, the president's pants were hung near an electric heater to dry. Later that day, the president discovered that part of his "lucky pants" was too close to the heater and had burned. He appeared extremely upset, and the staff and I tried our best to help. We learned later the president had kept those trousers for more than thirty-five years and made sure he always had them for fishing trips. Although we could not fix those pants, the president was soon joking again with his staff. I do recall that the boss continued to have good luck fishing, even without his "lucky pants."

&

Another fishing story I remember about President Roosevelt was at a fishing party on the Chesapeake Bay. There was a contest to see who would catch the first, the longest, and the heaviest fish. The president even offered prizes of five-dollar bills and a carton of cigarettes. One member of the party, a general as I recall, seemed to have a big catch and began boasting about earning all the prizes in one catch. When he finally reeled it in, it was not a fish but an old worn mattress. Everyone laughed, especially the boss, who repeated his famous words when in a good mood: "I love it, I love it. . . ."

&

Just a few hours' drive from Washington, DC, Shangri-La—now Camp David—is a few miles northeast of the little town of Thurmont in Maryland. Serving the president at Shangri-La, I lived with the other Filipino stewards in a cabin that the boss named "Little Luzon." My fellow stewards and I were truly grateful for this name because it recalled the country of our birth. The president's cabin was called the "Bear's Den." I can easily remember standing on the president's porch; I was surrounded by picturesque scenery. This cabin had a spacious living room, four bedrooms, and a kitchen. Every room contained a fireplace, which was very useful during cold weather because there was no central heating system. In the president's cabin, servicing the big fireplace was my responsibility. During cold weather, I kept the fire burning steadily to ensure warmth throughout the house.

The fishing was also very good there. President Roosevelt and his guests always caught beautiful trout during their stay. Among President Roosevelt's frequent guests at Shangri-La was Prime Minister Winston Churchill. They went fishing together quite often, usually in the morning. Of course, I helped the president with everything he needed. When he and his guest found an appropriate spot, I left them alone so they could fish and discuss the fate of the world undisturbed. When they caught enough fish or exhausted their subject of conversation, I was called to come help the president back to the camp.

On one of these occasions, I was an active witness to a rare disagreement between the president of the United States and the prime minister of His Majesty of Great Britain. The president told me he wanted his trout dipped in melted butter, rolled in cornmeal, cooked, and served with sliced lemon. When the boss finished giving me his culinary instructions, the prime minister told me with great emphasis that he thought the trout should be boiled with a little salt and sliced onions. I felt it was my responsibility to find a solution to this conflict between the leaders of the two greatest democracies in the world. I simply served these world leaders their two differently prepared trout dishes with toast and muffins. My boss and his guest seemed to enjoy having their trout fixed to their very own specifications. I was happy that my preparation and serving plan was successful. After their meal, I lit the prime minister's special cigar with a candle and then went into another room to put out the flame (at his request).

ᙍᕽ

I was with President Roosevelt on his second, third, and fourth campaigns for the presidency on his campaign train. Each time, we covered practically every state in the Union. While the boss was speaking on the platform of the rear car, I always stood behind him with a glass and a pitcher of cold water, ready to assist him in any way. I well remember another role I had at each of the campaign stops. A few minutes before each stop, I would assist the president in changing in and out of his clothing to put his leg braces on, and then take them back off after his speeches. The president was always pleasant during these unspoken but necessary details.

Once, after a campaign speech, I went down into the crowd and could hear a man telling the people who attended that this president was a godsend to America. He spoke about the creation of the Civilian Conservation Corps and went on and on about President Roosevelt. As I listened to this improvised speech of a man in the crowd, I understood why the American people elected the boss for president again and again.

෴

Even after serving President Roosevelt for twelve years, all of my recollections of the first lady could be summarized in just a few words. Mrs. Roosevelt was such a friendly, caring person. She was constantly busy doing something for others, and always had room for an extra person at her table. I remember how respected, loved, and good-natured she was. Whether in the White House or on the presidential yacht, retreat, or train, Mrs. Roosevelt was warm and kind to everyone around her; everyone felt at ease in her presence.

෴

The president and Mrs. Roosevelt always gave a Christmas party for the White House staff. The party was held in the East Room, and the guests would get in line to be greeted by President Roosevelt and the First Lady. There were tables with refreshments and different gifts. My children each received a personal gift bought especially for them. I received a Christmas card with money, and my wife received a fruit cake. All the staff members' families received cornucopias of candy. President Roosevelt and the First Lady never seemed hurried, creating a relaxing and warm atmosphere for all who attended.

෴

When their Royal Majesties the King and Queen of England were in Washington, DC, in 1939, the president gave a luncheon in their honor on the presidential yacht, the USS *Potomac*. A question quickly arose that became a long and tense conference between the protocol specialists of both governments, but they could not find a way to satisfy both countries. Who would be served first? King George VI and Queen Elizabeth, or President Roosevelt and our First Lady? I overheard their desperate and endless discussion and offered a simple suggestion. As the royal and presidential couples were seated at the same table, the president and king could be served at the same time; Mrs. Roosevelt and the queen could then be served together. My suggestion was welcomed, and the royal party was a great success. I knew this because, during the luncheon, I received a smiling glance of approval from the boss. I was later commended by the president for my service on this trip.

᪥

In the days ahead, the war presented a dark picture in the world and in the life of my boss. The Nazis were advancing everywhere; the Japanese were maintaining their strong push all over the Pacific. The only encouraging signal came from the US Navy in June of 1942. They stopped and defeated a Japanese fleet at Midway Islands.

During this time, I was with the president at Hyde Park for a few days. It was not a time of rest for him; the boss continued to work every day until late into the night. One night, after a summer storm followed by strong winds, I was doing my nightly duties for President Roosevelt. It was after midnight, and while I massaged his legs before he went to sleep for the night, we heard a noise coming from the porch near his bedroom. My boss seemed very concerned and told me to go out and investigate. I rushed out at once and looked around, but I did not find anything suspicious. I went back and told the president that there was no cause to worry; it was probably the wind.

The following morning, as I was making the president's bed, I found a silver-plated pistol under his pillow. I did not say a word to the boss. When he realized I had discovered the small weapon, I knew that was another secret I would keep. From that moment on, the president kept this little charged pistol with him everywhere he stayed. At the time, I could not understand why he felt he needed this little weapon. As president of the United States and commander in chief, he was constantly surrounded by Secret Service men and military guards. Even the Hyde Park mansion was surrounded by a strong military unit.

My silent perplexity did not last long. Shortly after my discovery, all the newspapers and radio stations announced the capture of a Nazi terrorist outfit. According to the news reports, they had been secretly brought into the United States by Hitler's submarines and had landed somewhere along the Florida coast. Two German submarines landed eight terrorists, who immediately scattered in the United States. I read all the details of these dangerous enemies in the newspapers. The terrorists were arrested before they could even start their mortal mission. When I finished reading, I fell on my knees and thanked God for having entrusted President Franklin Roosevelt with the charge of protecting the United States and saving the freedom of the world. My thoughts turned to the little silver-plated pistol; my eyes filled with tears. This great man, who could not leave his bed without help, was determined and ready to face the most dangerous gangsters in history and to defend this country at all costs. This incident gave me even more insight to understand the greatness of the president that destiny had ordered me to serve.

೧

The following year, November 1943, the president and his party were aboard the USS *Potomac.* Anchored at the navy yard, the ship immediately got underway for Quantico, Virginia. The staff and crew were not informed where we were headed beyond Quantico, not even me. We served sandwiches and refreshments as usual. The boss said that night, "We better turn in early so we can have an early start tomorrow." We did not know what this meant, but of course, my colleagues and I just obeyed orders.

I remember how, early the next morning, my fellow stewards and I did not ask questions as the yacht (somewhere in the Chesapeake Bay) pulled up alongside the big battleship USS *Iowa*. The presidential party and staff, along with the chiefs of staff of the armed forces, transferred to that ship; I was proud that the Filipino stewards were part of that group. Upon completion of the transfer, the presidential yacht and its escort of some destroyers got underway; they rapidly moved away from us in the early morning mist. Aboard the *Iowa,* we continued to serve and assist this elite group as we always did.

We served the presidential party their first meal aboard that day. The boss spent a quiet afternoon working on his papers, reading the newspapers, and listening to the radio. There was a cocktail party that evening, and after dinner, a movie was presented in the president's quarters.

Soon after midnight, the enormous battleship, escorted by three destroyers, moved toward the open sea. I learned then our next stop would be in Oran, French Algeria. We would cross the ocean and meet an old acquaintance, the Honorable Winston Churchill.

(I learned after our return from this long trip that the *Potomac* continued to cruise in the Chesapeake Bay up to our homecoming. Whoever spotted her had to believe the president was aboard his yacht.)

On just the second day crossing the Atlantic Ocean, a terrifying incident occurred that impacted everyone aboard. It started with an air defense drill. During this hypothetical air attack, I was standing, as usual, behind President Roosevelt's wheelchair. He watched with great curiosity from the deck just outside of his quarters. All of the guns of the anti-aircraft battery of the *Iowa* fired live ammunition. Although our ears were stuffed with cotton, the noise was still deafening. The boss seemed content observing the drill as commander in chief.

All of a sudden, the entire presidential party and crew heard a terrible explosion from under the water. There was no time for questions while the loudspeaker blared, "This ain't no drill!" The wake of a torpedo heading in our direction was detected by the *Iowa's* lookouts. The huge dreadnaught immediately increased its speed to thirty-one knots and started zigzagging. I saw a torpedo passing some twelve hundred yards astern the ship with a frightening speed. Our ship turned sharply. Someone muttered, "Nazi submarine." I heard my boss whisper, "Oh my goodness."

At this time, I was still standing with the president and could feel the unbearable tension and panic around him and on every corner of the ship. Like in a dream, I can never forget the expressions of the heads of the army, navy, and air force of our nation at war. As for myself, I had a strange feeling. I am not a coward; I am not a hero, yet still I was not afraid. It was my job to assist and protect the president. While the deadly torpedo was rushing toward us, my whole life seemed to flash before me. From my childhood in my native Filipino village, to my precious wife and children, and then to this moment. I was standing behind the president of the United States of America, the supreme leader of a free world struggling for survival. I was absolutely sure I would be able to save him.

Then, as suddenly as it started, the tension lifted. The stray fully armed torpedo disappeared into the sea, taking its uncertainty with it. Fear turned into calm aboard the ship. We finally learned what happened. During the drill, there was an accidental firing by one of our escorting destroyers. The skipper on that destroyer must have carried a great burden after discovering the president of the United States and the chiefs of staff of the army, navy, and air force were aboard the ship he had almost destroyed. Without the quick maneuvering of the *Iowa* crew, history may have been written differently.

By Friday, November 19, 1943, we were passing the Strait of Gibraltar; we reached Oran the following morning on a beautiful day, as I remember it. We disembarked at the famous port of Mers-el-Kebir. The president was greeted by two of his sons Colonel Roosevelt and Lieutenant Franklin Roosevelt Jr., as well as General Dwight Eisenhower and other officers. We stayed two days in this area of North Africa while the president visited battlefields by plane, met with visitors, and worked. Then, the presidential party traveled by air to Cairo. The boss stayed at a place called Mena Villa, the home of an ambassador, during this trip.

I arrived with the other stewards to Cairo ahead of the president, so we had a good opportunity to prepare the villa for the boss. The house was completely furnished with all kinds of international drinks, cigars, and cigarettes. There was a yard with a variety of the most beautiful flowers. The ambassador who lived here asked me to place a fresh-cut rose in a small flower vase every day in his study in memory of his late mother. I fulfilled his request during our entire stay in Cairo.

The boss met with Prime Minister Churchill in this house, along with other leaders, both military and diplomatic. I recall Generalissimo Chiang Kai-Shek and his wife visiting the president with their great Chinese delegation. They held many conferences, and I observed that Madame Chiang always sat beside her husband and served as his interpreter. During all of these meetings, my fellow Filipino stewards and I served refreshments, sandwiches, cigars, and cigarettes.

There were many other famous visitors. I was there when Mr. Vishinsky, the Soviet minister, paid a visit to President Roosevelt. I served the Soviet minister with my usual impassive expression. I also recall visits from the Turkish president, King George II of Greece, King Peter II of Yugoslavia, and members of the Egyptian government.

On November 25, the boss organized a Thanksgiving Dinner for his entire party and British guests. The turkeys were brought from Washington. The president enjoyed carving the turkey for his guests. He grew tired after filling four or five dinner plates, so I picked up the turkey platter and took it back to the kitchen where the chef finished carving. At this dinner, we served light and dark wines, sparkling burgundy, and champagne. Wonderful toasts were exchanged between the leaders; I was grateful to listen to the words of these amazing figures in history.

❧

We left Cairo by plane and headed toward Tehran. As the plane passed over Jerusalem, I unexpectedly recalled my dear mother mentioning this place in her prayers when I was just a young boy. I prayed and thanked God silently.

At first, we stayed at the American Embassy. I was prepared to serve Marshal Joseph Stalin at a dinner that was offered by my boss; however, this dinner never took place because I learned Stalin declined the president's invitation. Stalin had sent a message that he would not attend because he was tired. I did not like this, but of course, I kept my opinion to myself. I also did not agree with the plan of moving from the American Embassy to the Russian Embassy in Tehran; however, it was argued that the great leaders should stay under the protection of the Russians in their own building.

I had an almost uneasy feeling when I first entered the building. There was a mass of Russian soldiers; they were quite different from the military service members I was familiar with. In the presence of those armed soldiers, I felt privileged to wear an American uniform, but for the first time in my navy career, I was homesick.

My comrades and I had quite the undertaking at the Russian Embassy—preparing a dinner for our boss and distinguished foreign guests in a room with, initially, no running water or stove. We were in a bad spot, and I thought, *How could they (our hosts) show us an empty room without anything in it and tell us this was the kitchen?* Thankfully, some of the army soldiers traveling with us installed a portable stove and supplied us with gallons of fresh water.

I must say that the Russian kitchen personnel tried to help us, but their leaders had forgotten the simple courtesy for hosts to provide at least one person who could help interpret. There was not one among them who understood English or even Spanish. As for my fellow Filipinos and I, we could not pronounce or understand one word in Russian. Since we had to communicate, we became creative in telling the Russian kitchen staff what we needed. We would show them utensils or plates, and then signal with our fingers how many we needed. This understanding was established between the two camps. We contributed to this working relationship by offering American chocolate and cigarettes to our Russian counterparts.

At the president's first meeting with Joseph Stalin, I served refreshments, cigars, and cigarettes. I immediately noted that Stalin did not take anything; he only puffed on his own pipe. During dinner later that day, I served all the guests as I normally did. As soon as I reached

Stalin, he glanced suspiciously at me and signaled with his index finger that he did not want anything to eat. I could feel his piercing look as I served the other guests sitting around the long table. At first, I thought that he did not like American food, or that he was not feeling well. I soon discovered this was not the case. A bodyguard entered with a strange platter of foods I did not recognize and placed it before his boss. Stalin started to eat with a good appetite. I could not believe that a guest refused to eat the food offered by his host and brought his own meal! Although he was sitting at the top of history with the other great leaders of the free world, this man's wariness would not let him eat the food that all the other guests were enjoying.

Stalin continued to keep an eye on me that evening. I could not understand his words, but I finally heard him say to his interpreter, "Yapanets . . . Yapanets!" The uneasy Russian general spoke to my boss, saying, "I hope this man is not a Japanese." Stalin pointed directly at me. When the boss heard this, he laughed heartily and told the interpreter to inform Stalin there was nothing to worry about. The president told the Soviet leader that I was a Filipino, son of an allied nation, and that I had worked for him for many years. Stalin seemed to be greatly relieved, and I was so glad the supreme leaders of the world could move on with their discussion of victory and a better future for suffering nations. I thought to myself, *What kind of man could imagine that the president of the United States would bring an enemy with him when he met other allied leaders?* Stalin continued to have his own food served during our remaining time in Tehran; however, he did enjoy our assorted homemade cookies, made by the Filipinos. He gladly accepted them—even from me.

{Describing this first dinner at the Soviet Embassy in Tehran, the *Log of the President's Trip to Africa and the Middle East, November—December 1943*, reads, "Note: Much credit is due to the President's Filipino messboys for the success of the dinner this evening. They prepared the entire meal under a real handicap. They had moved into a virtually empty room at the Russian Embassy at 4:00 p.m. Ranges and much kitchen equipment had first to be installed before they could even begin the preparation of the meal. But with their resourcefulness they saw it done and came through with the meal in their usual fine style."}

Commander William Rigdon (1962, p. 6) also mentioned this dinner, specifically about the Filipinos, in his book *White House Sailor*: "I was early put in charge of the wonderful Filipino stewards from the Presidential yacht who always accompanied the President away from Washington to prepare and serve his meals, and also the big luncheons and dinners he often gave. They were loyal. They were tireless. Often they were sleepless—and always they worked silently. . . . They could do anything. A few hours after landing, with no stove in the kitchen, and no cooking utensils either, they served a grand state dinner at Teheran(sic)."}

℘

The tension of this first day at the Russian Embassy in Tehran subsided, despite a rough beginning. After that first dinner, I served liquor and demitasse; the conversation between President Roosevelt, Stalin, Churchill, and others lasted well into the night.

When the guests left, I took the boss to his room. I started to prepare his bed while he sat in an armchair. Suddenly, the president became very sick. His face turned pale and he was sweating and groaning. I ran to his side, but I was so worried that words could not come out of my mouth. I was terrified since I had never seen him look like that. We were not at home, not even in our own embassy covered by our national flag. With a trembling hand, I reached for the telephone and called the president's physician. He rushed in with attendants who provided great care to the suffering president. His discomfort was soon over. The doctor explained that the symptoms were the unexpected consequence of physical exhaustion. I was relieved to see the boss falling asleep peacefully, but I did not leave his room until I was sure he was alright. Thankfully, the president woke up well the next morning, but I will never forget that day in Tehran.

℘

On our way back to Washington aboard the battleship *Iowa*, I heard the presidential party discuss some of the historical figures they had met. One name I recall in that discussion was Madame Chiang Kai-Shek. I am sorry to reveal she was not very popular in and around the White House during World War II. While President Roosevelt and the First Lady always treated the staff with dignity and respect, this First Lady of China signaled the personnel of the presidential household by hand clapping. I know this may have been appropriate while in her home country, but I do not believe that it was fitting in the White House. She had some other habits that did not fit into the strict wartime austerity in the White House. Even the boss had one egg instead of his usual two eggs for breakfast or lunch. Madame made it clear that she wanted two eggs at a time. She also brought her own silk sheets, which needed to be changed every morning.

❧

I frequently observed that President Roosevelt was a man who was very careful not to waste anything. Once, I was with him in a motorboat while he was fishing a short distance from our ship. The sea became rough, and suddenly a big wave tossed water inside our boat. A pack of cigarettes that was near the president's seat was drenched in water. I reached for the cigarettes to throw them into the sea, but the boss stopped me. When we returned to the ship, I saw the president, sitting in his wheelchair on the deck, spreading out the cigarettes to dry. During the shortages of World War II, I even remember President Roosevelt being sure not to waste any toothpaste when he dropped some out of the tube.

❧

As a rule, President Roosevelt never discussed politics or state affairs with me, despite the fact that I spent so much time with him during his entire presidency. However, one day, I believe in 1944, the president told me about one of his planned political actions. He knew most Filipinos were Catholic, including me. One morning as I assisted him during his daily routine, he told me he decided to send a Cardinal on a special mission to Rome to meet with the Pope. I told the boss, "That would be wonderful, Mr. President." He seemed to be pleased with my reaction to this confidential communication.

☙

I was with President Roosevelt on his last Christmas at Hyde Park, the place where he was born over sixty years earlier. It was during the Christmas season of 1944; the entire Roosevelt family was there, as usual. The president had lost a lot of weight since last summer, and his appetite was not the same. The boss remained cheerful, especially when surrounded by his grandchildren.

When Christmas Eve came, there was a gathering around the big Christmas tree; there was a nice gift for everyone, including family members and every attendant of the presidential household. The president was very excited when he opened his presents. I remember there was a pile of woolen socks under the tree, and someone suggested giving a few pairs to the grounds superintendent. The boss replied with a wink, "I want to save them all and give them to him next Christmas." President Roosevelt continued to open the packages with care, saving the ribbons and wrapping paper. He looked at me and said, "I hope I shall be able to use this next Christmas." Fascinated by his memorable face, I silently uttered an anxious prayer that it should be so. . . .

☙

The morning after his fourth inauguration in January 1945, I went into the president's room and found him sitting up in his bed. I had to make an effort to hide from him how shocked I was by his physical appearance. He looked pale and thin, and his hands trembled, yet he was very pleasant. When I picked up the morning paper with his picture on the cover page, the boss graciously signed it for me. This was the last autograph given to me by this great president.

Newspaper copy signed by FDR

ℭ⅋ℑ

I did not go with President Roosevelt to Yalta at the end of January 1945, because I was on leave. When the president returned home the next month, I was again on duty in the White House. My anxiety about the president's health grew as I observed his deteriorating physical state. He seemed to be completely exhausted, and I only occasionally saw a smile on his tired face.

I heard for the last time his famous laugh when I unpacked his suitcase, brought back from Yalta and Cairo. In one of his trunks, I found a richly embroidered Arabic costume. With a smile, the boss told me it was a gift from King Saud to Mrs. Roosevelt. I saw a twinkle in the president's eyes; he was going to use the gift to play a joke on his wife. I learned later that he simply handed it to the first lady without saying a word. He was so exhausted during the last days of his life.

ℭ⅋ℑ

During his last vacation at Hyde Park, I realized the president was a very sick man. Since I was his personal attendant, with him early in the morning to late evening, I watched him gradually lose control over his whole body. I continued to wheel him to the dining room, where members of the family were always waiting for him. By this time, he hardly touched any food, while in the past he ate everything put before him. It was a tragic sight for me to see as he held a big cup of coffee, half-filled, so he would not spill it; this was his only nourishment.

My boss continued his old routine, but every day at a slower pace. One morning, he scared me because he slept much longer than ever before. In my worry, I checked on him several times in his bedroom and watched his slow and irregular breathing. The signs of total exhaustion remained on his pale face as he slept. He finally woke up.

As we returned to Washington by train, the president himself granted me leave, telling me I looked tired, and I should take a little rest. He left for Warm Springs, Georgia, where he intended to spend some vacation time. I was not with President Roosevelt during his final moments. When his car pulled out from the White House driveway, I could not imagine, in spite of all my anxieties, that I was seeing my boss for the last time.

෴

On April 12, 1945, I was sitting in my living room when the radio announced President Roosevelt had passed away. This information stunned the entire world, but there are no words that can describe the feelings of a man who spent twelve years of his life with this extraordinary human being. I would remember him as a giant among men, whose greatness completely concealed his crippled body and whose kindness was also a manifestation of his greatness.

I rushed immediately to the White House and waited there until his body arrived from Warm Springs. For a long time, I stood there, before his open coffin. He looked thirty years younger. Suddenly, I felt a touch on my arm. It was the president's daughter, Mrs. Anna Roosevelt-Boettiger. She whispered, "I know how you feel, Isaac."

Every day, I had seen the crippled body of this great president, but I could never see him as a crippled man. From the first day in his service, I was astounded by his superhuman strength, which invigorated not only his nation, but everyone who had the privilege to work with him. As for his influence on the entire nation, it is not my task, but that of historians, to describe it.

✧

After President Roosevelt's burial in the flower garden of Hyde Park, I received my orders to stay in the White House for a month to assist with packing and moving the Roosevelt family's belongings. This was a difficult job for me. Even after seeing the president's body lying in the casket, I was unable, for several days, to realize he had left the White House forever. His voice that had called me so often throughout the past twelve years had become silent for eternity.

Mrs. Roosevelt came often to supervise as my colleagues and I packed, and I admired her compassion after this terrible tragedy. Poor little Fala felt like me. This little dog had a human soul. The president's pet wandered aimlessly in and around the White House, and I am absolutely sure he hoped to see his master coming. . . .

✧

As for me, I felt a chapter in my life was closed, yet my heart was filled with gratitude. I often wondered at the miracle of God that was my destiny. No matter what would happen to me in my remaining years, I felt I had not lived in vain.

(I had the opportunity to go to Hyde Park after President Roosevelt's death. Mrs. Roosevelt spent a long time visiting with me and took me to President Roosevelt's grave.)

CHAPTER 4

A Glimpse with President and Mrs. Truman (1945–1952)

Human beings never know today what the next day will bring to them. . . .

During that month of moving, I was not yet in service of the new president. I saw him several times, and he seemed to be the same friendly man I knew as a senator and vice president. I heard that it took him some time to realize Harry S. Truman was now the president of the United States. It was not easy for him to suddenly give up his long walks in the city. I heard that one day he tried to take a walk alone when exiting the car, but he was immediately surrounded by news reporters. Another day, he caused real despair to the Secret Service because he left the White House alone and walked to his bank in downtown Washington. Many people immediately gathered around the building because everyone wanted to see President Truman. After that incident, the president never left the White House alone.

After fifteen historic and exciting years in the service of two Presidents of the United States, I began my service aboard the USS *Augusta*. I was again chief steward aboard a beautiful warship of Uncle Sam. On July 7, 1945, President Harry S. Truman and his party came aboard. I learned the *Augusta* would soon sail to Europe, where the president was scheduled to meet with Prime Minister Winston Churchill and Marshal Joseph Stalin. I learned afterward Antwerp in Belgium was our destination. The president would fly from there to Potsdam, near Berlin, to meet with the other two world leaders. I still thought then that this trip was only an unexpected addition to my extraordinary life story thus far. At the end of this trip, I thought I would live the rest of my years remembering only the past two presidents. Of course, I was again wrong, but I did not know this then.

I have never compared my commanders in chief; I have simply observed their similarities and differences. In my intimate service to the presidents, one thing I have learned and know for sure is human beings preserve their personal character even when they reach the top of society. I believe President Hoover was naturally dignified. Though extremely kind with everyone around him, he always seemed to keep to himself. President Roosevelt was physically unable to move around, but in his unfortunate immobility he spread the radiation of his glowing personality. He was a giant among men, whose greatness completely concealed his crippled body. At first sight, President Truman made an absolutely different impression on me than the former presidents I had served. This boss was like some good neighbor of yours, whose friendly persona and down-to-earth energy added to the natural dignity of the president of the United States.

While aboard the *Augusta*, the new boss stayed in the admiral's stateroom; he went there only to sleep or for some important conferences with his aides. Early one morning, after our first night crossing the Atlantic Ocean, I could not believe my eyes when I saw the president briskly walking on the deck. Each time he met an officer or seaman, he stopped and chatted with them. I even saw President Truman take a seaman's white cap and put it on his own head. He began to wear it frequently while on the deck.

I don't know whether it was a good thing or not, but there were no news reporters on the ship. I have to add that, within the first hour aboard the *Augusta*, President Truman gave orders that no crew member aboard should come to attention when he met the president. This resulted in the officers and sailors naturally talking to the commander in chief, but their respect toward him was even greater than it was before this supreme order was given.

I witnessed President Truman's friendly nature daily while on the ship. He visited all of the officers and seamen, even eating lunch with them. He refused to be served at a table, and he followed the self-service waiting line with his tray in hand. When he had time, the president stayed with the sailors to talk, asking them about their families, homes, and sweethearts. He signed many cards to be mailed home. I remember this commander in chief got word that a seaman on board shared his last name. After researching and discovering they were related, President Truman called the seaman into his office and told him he could call him Uncle Harry. (I do not believe he ever did, but the other seamen greatly admired this young navy service member.)

This commander in chief also came to visit the seamen in the sick bay, offering kind words and telling jokes to lighten their load; this definitely helped with recovery and lifted the seamen's spirits. After all, it was not very common for sick enlisted men on the ship to be visited by the president of the United States.

What a strange and comforting new thing it was for me to see the boss, the president of the United States, constantly in motion with the intention of making personal connections. I remember President Truman playing shuffleboard or medicine ball with the officers on the *Augusta*. The boss even went down to the boiler room, and the men working there had the privilege and pleasure to talk a little with their commander in chief.

I believe every action and gesture of President Truman was a lesson of history for us. Here was living proof that in the American democracy, the presidency has nothing to do with birthright or other social privileges, but it is the right of any citizen who is qualified by his talents and honesty. What fascinated me about this president was his simplicity in greatness. It is very easy for a simple man to be simple, but to remain simple when one is president of the United States is a manifest sign of greatness.

I remember seeing this greatness one day when the president stood before a picture of the late President Roosevelt that hung in one of the halls of the ship. The current commander in chief said, "Here is one of the greatest men in history, and I am unable to fill his shoes." I was deeply touched by his words, although I believed he, too, was one of the greatest men in history.

❧

As the *Augusta* approached the English Channel, I observed traces of the great war. These traces of the war's terrible destruction were everywhere. There were still floating mines in the channel and the wreckage of sunken ships. We were soon before the port of Antwerp in Belgium. Thousands of people cheered for President Truman from the shores. I also saw the silent crowd of German war prisoners behind barbed fences. . . .

Many Allied high-ranking officers and civilian authorities came aboard to pay their respects to the president. After these visits, President Truman and his party disembarked and went to a military airfield to take the presidential plane to Potsdam. My colleagues and I stayed aboard, and the *Augusta* was again underway in the direction of Plymouth, England. We were ordered to wait for the presidential party there.

About two weeks later, President Truman was back aboard the *Augusta*. The British battleship *Renown* waited nearby with King George VI aboard. Following a short visit with His Majesty, the president soon received the British king aboard our ship. I remember the beautiful, historic ceremony that is customary when the heads of state of naval powers visit each other aboard their respective flagships.

A major event of our trip aboard the *Augusta* occurred shortly thereafter, in August of 1945. President Truman was sitting and eating his lunch with us when an officer brought him a radio message. His relaxed countenance changed, and he became very serious. I watched the president while he spoke. With indescribable tension, the commander in chief told us the atomic bomb was dropped on the Japanese city of Hiroshima. He added, "It is the greatest thing in history. It is time for us to get home." At that moment, I felt I was standing with him on behalf of the American people, who hate war and want peace.

The *Augusta* finally moored at Newport News, Virginia, and President Truman and his party immediately took the presidential train back to Washington.

C/S

A few weeks later, I received my new orders. I was assigned to be at the service of President Harry S. Truman wherever he needed me. I was assigned to serve him mostly aboard the presidential yacht *Williamsburg*; at the Little White House in Key West, Florida; and during his travels across the country.

The second half of 1945 was a tumultuous period both in the nation and the president's life. The most terrible of wars was over, yet peace did not seem to come. The country struggled with all the problems of transitioning from war to peace, and every unsolved problem seemed to land directly on the desk of the new president of the United States in the White House.

Because of this, the boss did not come aboard the *Williamsburg* until the end of that year. From every viewpoint, the USS *Williamsburg* was a ship worthy to be used by the president of the United States. The ship was tied up at the Naval Gun Factory on the Anacostia River, in Washington, DC. Prior to this, the crew did an excellent job making the yacht spotless both inside and out. Every stateroom, the presidential lounge, dining room, and the president's quarters were decorated with beautiful historical pictures. The dining room was large enough for twenty-four guests, and it included a fireplace. The china service was specially designed for the presidential yacht; each piece was trimmed with blue and gold and stamped with the presidential seal. Francis I silverware was used for dining. Finally, there were two pianos aboard, one in the presidential lounge and another in the dining room.

President Truman came aboard to inspect the yacht for the first time in November 1945. He came with his naval aide and several members of his White House staff. The boss was pleased with everything and warmly congratulated the commanding officer. The crew members were waiting for the president at their designated stations. He had a kind word for each of them. As chief steward, my station was inside of the presidential quarters. It was my responsibility to ensure these quarters were always in tip-top shape. What an honor it was to show the boss his quarters and to receive his kind words. He especially liked the pianos that were located in the presidential lounge and dining room and ran his fingers over the keys of both of them. I had the privilege of hearing him play many times after that while I was busy in his quarters. (I discovered he liked to play the piano for himself when he was alone; those were peaceful moments amidst his tremendous work and responsibilities.)

After this first inspection, the presidential party enjoyed a cruise down the Potomac River to the Mattawoman Channel. My fellow stewards and I served refreshments and lunch aboard. It was always a pleasure to see the president of the United States relaxing and enjoying himself aboard the ship. The boss told many good jokes. We returned to the navy yard before dark, and the presidential party went back to the White House.

{Another piano story: I heard this from White House attendants who went with the boss to San Francisco for the opening assembly of the United Nations in June 1945. The president traveled by air, and his plane was followed by another one with White House correspondents. The president stopped in Washington state to visit an old friend, the governor and former senator. The news reporters were quite nervous because they had not yet established a routine relationship with the new president; they did not want to miss any story they could cover surrounding him.

As for President Truman, he was not yet accustomed to certain hardships of his office and tried to maintain his privacy. That night, during his visit, President Truman left the governor's mansion by himself. No one realized he had left, and he went straight to the state capitol and sat before the organ in the assembly hall. He began to play some melodies alone, or so he thought. A few minutes later, a group of sleepy correspondents rushed into the assembly hall, where they found the president playing the organ.)

❧

Aboard the *Williamsburg*, the president was just as friendly with officers as he was with the enlisted men on the ship. I once again observed him walking around the ship, talking to the sailors. If there was a new crew member, the president always asked him how long he had been in service, how he liked his duty, and if he was satisfied with the food. I thought this was a kind thing to do because every new sailor started working with a certain anxiety knowing the commander in chief was also aboard the ship. This simple act of kindness toward the enlisted men dissolved their anxiety and created a deep respect and devotion toward the boss.

President Truman's warm and caring nature was also extended to the ship's barber, who grew to love the president. Each time the boss had a haircut, he pulled out a brand-new dollar from his pocket, autographed it, and gave it to the barber. I was sure he never spent these precious dollar bills signed by the president of the United States. After his time of service aboard, the happy barber succeeded in accumulating a piece of history.

I observed that President Truman was always very generous with the personnel who assisted him. One day, he sent a shirt to the yacht's laundry service, and the serviceman found a one-hundred-dollar bill in the shirt pocket. He immediately rushed to the president and gave him back his lost money. The boss thanked him with a great big smile, a warm handshake, and ten crisp, autographed one-dollar bills.

ल

President Truman enjoyed many weekends and cruises aboard the presidential yacht. Most of the time he was surrounded by a group of his closest friends. They played cards quite often. It was an interesting thing to watch the boss play poker. I observed the complete opposite of President Roosevelt's winning streaks; President Truman was almost always the underdog in the game. He was a determined, stubborn player, who never gave up until he got some even break. One day, while they were engaged in a poker battle, one of the guests brought in a carefully wrapped package. He opened it and revealed a picture of eight different dogs playing a poker game. The boss was clearly amused by this picture, knowing the stubborn bulldog represented his own playing tactics.

It was during these social games that I also discovered President Truman could write equally well with both his right and left hands. He demonstrated this unusual skill to his guests, writing his presidential signature with both hands.

☙

Since the beginning of my long service to the presidents, I had become accustomed to the solemn faces and behavior of most of the people who had the honor of giving advice to the chief executive. I observed that the president was usually the one who broke the ice during long conferences and meetings.

I can recall one particularly tense conference aboard the *Williamsburg* in December of 1945. What surprised me was that President Truman was the most serious among all the gentlemen at the long table. I could sense something was wrong, but I continued my duties serving refreshments, emptying ashtrays, and seeing where I was needed. Although I was to pay no attention to these highly official and secret conversations, I was concerned to see my boss so serious and absorbed in thought.

The following day was filled with presidential conferences, and I received orders to make preparations for the president's meeting with the secretary of state. He had returned from Moscow, and from the newspaper headlines, I understood that he had met with Stalin. When the secretary met privately with the president in the stateroom, the boss told me in an unusually stern voice, "Don't let anybody disturb us!"

I could not forget the tense atmosphere of this presidential cruise; it preoccupied my mind for a time, but I eventually forgot about it. It would be much later that I learned the historical events which occurred that December concerning the secretary and the Soviet dictator. From the big headlines in the newspapers, I realized that important negotiations had taken place during that time aboard the *Williamsburg*.

ↄ

The Filipino staff accompanied President Truman to the Little White House in Key West, Florida. We followed the orders given with great diligence:

> *It is imperative that all stewards present a neat and orderly appearance at all times. It is also imperative that the Little White House (and Quarters L) be kept spotless at all times. After each Captain's Inspection, Chief Esperancilla will take immediate action to correct any discrepancies as a result of the inspection in the Little White House . . . Chief Esperancilla will be in charge and directly responsible (to Lieutenant Commander Roberts) for the smooth and efficient operation of the Little White House.*

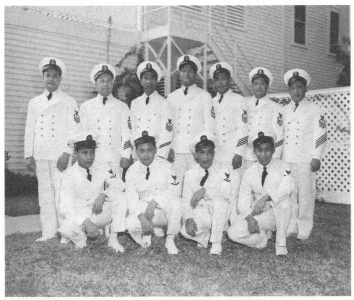

Fillipino staff at Key West; Chief Esperancilla standing second from left

A typical morning routine for President Truman at Key West started with an early wakeup around seven thirty in the morning. (At other places, aboard the *Williamsburg*, on trips, and the White House, the

Chief Esperancilla standing first on the left

president woke up a little earlier, between six and seven o'clock in the morning). He took his first of two baths of the day. He brushed his teeth with table salt and water. When I asked him why he used salt and water, he explained that he learned it when he was a little boy at the family farm in Missouri. His saltwater gargle was followed by a shot of whiskey and a glass of orange juice. He got dressed quickly and neatly.

Before breakfast, the president went on a thirty- to sixty-minute morning walk with members of his staff or guests (and Secret Service men, of course). When they returned from the promenade, the boss drank his first cup of coffee and held a discussion with his aides while waiting for breakfast. He was always very pleasant, telling many jokes to his guests around the table. President Truman's breakfast regularly consisted of a grapefruit, one poached egg, two slices of crispy bacon, Melba toast, and a second cup of coffee. The president always ate the entire pulp of the grapefruit. He told me, "The grapefruit pulp is very good for the teeth." While the gentlemen were eating, I placed the morning papers on a stand at the president's side. He would glance at the headlines and pick up the paper that interested him the most. After breakfast, the president began his work, filled with studying documents, making dictations, and meetings.

While at Key West, the presidential party would leave the Little White House and walk to the president's private beach on the base. President Truman enjoyed being at the beach. I would be waiting for them with all the beach supplies, including refreshments and cigarettes. After swimming and playing medicine ball or other outdoor games, whoever was thirsty would find me ready to serve.

On the return trip to the Little White House, the president often drove the car himself. I am sure the boss would have liked very much to go into town to see all the curious tourists that were there, but the Secret Service was opposed to this. This is one of the disadvantages of being president, especially when one is such a friendly person as President Harry S. Truman. Back at his quarters, the boss got back to his work.

A light lunch was served shortly after we returned to the Little White House. As always, I made sure the president's meat was well done, just as he liked it. Lunch was followed by a conference or meeting with his advisers. The president then relaxed by fishing, sunbathing, or taking a short nap.

My boss continued to work through the rest of the day, reading, writing, signing papers, and conferencing until dinner. I served cocktails around six thirty in the evening, followed by dinner. If President Truman was away from the First Lady and his daughter, he would call them for a long chat. The boss never missed these long-distance calls to his wife and daughter when he was away on trips. The day ended with a movie or card game with the president's advisers and guests. He then held a final conference to prepare for the next day.

At the end of the day, before going to bed, I observed President Truman washing his socks (and sometimes even his underwear) each night. At first, I protested and told him that this was my job. "No, my friend," he answered me, "my mother taught me when I was a child that this is a job which must be done by every person himself." Before completely ending his day and getting his well-deserved rest, President Truman again brushed his teeth with saltwater.

c/o

One day at Key West, President Truman, the First Lady, and Miss Truman received eighteen guests at an outdoor luncheon. As chief steward, I had the responsibility of organizing the tables and the entire service. With the stewards in my charge, we placed near every chair a small serving table. On each table, we arranged the silverware, salt and pepper, glasses, napkins, and ashtrays. When the food was spread out on the decorated long table, I inspected everything again. I went back to the house and announced, "Mr. President, the luncheon is served." Everyone came out, including the hosts and guests, and stood behind their chairs waiting for the president to take his seat.

After the boss took his seat, an unusual accident happened. (I think this was the only one of its kind during my long service with four presidents). I was standing with my fellow stewards when, to my horror, after everyone sat down, I saw one of the guests, who was a rather big and tall man, miss his chair by a few inches. I rushed immediately to help him up, but because of his size, I had a hard time.

As I struggled to get him up, the other stewards came to help. The president's daughter started to laugh, and soon everyone, including the boss, was also laughing. Trying not to laugh ourselves, we finally got this guest seated. Although he was embarrassed, he laughed too. Despite this incident, the luncheon was a great success. I am also sure the warm atmosphere that always surrounded President Truman and his family made everything turn out well.

c/o

I remember receiving a kind invitation from my boss one evening at the Little White House in Key West. I was busy arranging the dining room and putting it back in order after a presidential reception. President Truman came in and said to me, "Chief, Miss Margaret will be on TV tonight; come in to watch her and tell the others to come too."

After completing my duties, I quickly went back to my quarters and told the rest of the Filipino staff. We were really excited, to say the least. At this time, watching TV was not yet a common activity. That night, the presidential living room was quite crowded; the president was sitting in the center facing the television set, surrounded by guests and other staff. The first lady sat quietly in an armchair with needlework in her hands while she watched both the screen and her husband. For me, the most interesting show was the boss; he kept his eyes on the TV, and his face was glowing.

છ્ય

When the President's daughter, Miss Truman, was around, she was the life of the presidential party. She always had a friendly smile, just like her father. She loved to eat outside and shared her father's taste in food and drink.

છ્ય

Another time I remember with the Truman family occurred when they were eating watermelon around the dinner table. Miss Truman started to flick watermelon seeds at her father, and the battle was on. The president scored on his daughter's nose and laughed heartily. After participating for a short time, the first lady ended the battle. Everybody obeyed the boss. For me, the president was the boss. For him, it was the first lady.

છ્ય

Mrs. Truman was always very quiet, and I did not ever hear her raise her voice with anyone. In her own quiet way, she was always able to express herself and communicate very well. It was touching to see how tenderly she was loved and respected by her charming daughter and powerful husband. When the president was in a conference with his assistants or other advisers, I would see Mrs. Truman reading in a corner of the room in a comfortable chair. She never participated in the general conversation, but the boss turned to her often with questions, and she answered with a smile. She remained unaffected if the atmosphere of the meeting became tense. For me, it was always a great pleasure to serve the kind Mrs. Truman, and I could not understand why some of the attendants were a little bit afraid of her. I think maybe her quietness made them a little uncertain of what to expect.

∾

During the summer of 1946, President Truman and the First Lady spent a weekend with their guests at Shangri-La. The presidential party enjoyed walking outdoors in the fresh mountain air, and everyone appeared to sleep well at the camp.

One night, the presidential couple was awakened by what they thought were footsteps on the rooftop. The boss, who was known for being a light sleeper, came out of the house in his pajamas telling the attendants, Secret Service men, and me to investigate. We all looked around the house, and the Secret Service men climbed up onto the roof. The president even looked for himself to find the cause of the strange noise. The branches of the trees were a good distance from the roof of the presidential cabin, so the sound of the footsteps remained a mystery. The president returned to his bedroom.

(Another "ghost story": After President Roosevelt's death, there had been stories circulating throughout Camp Shangri-La that the main lodge was haunted. Some of the young American and Filipino seamen believed these stories and were afraid to be alone in the lodge. The older stewards and I knew better, but we let the joke go on. The ghost was a string tied to the rocking chair of a former guest, causing the chair to gently rock back and forth. I am not sure which of the Shangri-La officers were responsible for this, but it was all in fun. This story, except for the string, eventually made it to one of the Washington newspapers.

As for President Truman's light sleeping habits, I heard another story from White House attendants about a storm. One night, a strong storm swept over Washington. President Truman woke up and worried that there may have been some windows left open in the White House.

Without waking up any personnel for assistance, the boss jumped out of his bed and rushed to take a tour of each of the rooms. He found several windows open and rainwater covering the floors. Soon, attendants came rushing in to mop up the water, but no one could convince the boss that this was not a job for the president of the United States.)

∞

In November of 1946, I had the unique privilege of serving refreshments to the president of the United States four hundred feet below the surface of the Atlantic Ocean. The navy had sent the former Nazi submarine *U-2513* (caught intact by our forces) to Key West for President Truman to inspect. The presidential party for this inspection was composed of an admiral, the chief economic adviser, and other White House staff members. The boss also took me with him. This was in and of itself an amazing experience to see the president of the United States aboard a warship, which a little more than a year ago was one of the most dangerous enemy weapons.

The commander in chief was welcomed aboard the former German submarine by its new commanding officer. I followed the president and his party as they inspected every corner of the ship. Then the submarine got underway and breakfast was served to the guests. I doubt that a presidential breakfast was ever served before in these conditions.

The *U-2513* progressed rapidly on the surface, and when it reached a designated point, the order was given for diving. For every guest, from the president down to me, this was a first and thrilling experience. In just a few minutes, we were four hundred and fifty feet below sea level. There, I served refreshments to the presidential party.

During those moments, I couldn't help but think what a difference time makes. Exactly three years earlier, I was aboard the *Iowa*, standing with President Roosevelt and his wheelchair. For a brief time, we thought that a Nazi submarine's torpedo was threatening to sink our ship. I clearly remember my feelings in those moments, how I was not scared for myself, but for the great President Roosevelt, who, though paralyzed, carried the threatened free world upon his shoulders. I recall praying and asking God to save him. Now, here we were in a captured Nazi submarine, and I was serving refreshments to a smiling president and his party.

After some silent depth cruising with the most precious passenger to ever be carried by a former enemy submarine, the ship climbed up to the surface. Soon after, the presidential party was back inside the Little White House in Key West.

I was with President Truman in December of the following year when the submarine returned to Key West. My boss was received with full honors as a qualified submariner and was presented with a scroll, making him an honorary commanding officer of the *U-2513*. He expressed his thanks in a touching and heartfelt speech and decorated four of the officers there.

℃

In May of 1947, President Miguel Aleman of Mexico visited Washington and was the guest of President Truman aboard the *Williamsburg*; they would make a trip down the Potomac River to Mount Vernon. Two days before the Mexican president arrived, blooming azaleas of the most beautiful colors were planted along the inner areas of the Naval Gun Factory. These were such a welcoming sight when the visiting foreign dignitaries passed through the Navy Yard toward the presidential yacht, which was moored on the Anacostia River.

I served as chief steward at the dinner aboard the *Williamsburg*. When the party was settled on the ship, the president of Mexico talked to me in Spanish. This was one of the rare occasions that my knowledge of Spanish was very useful. That, I believe, made this visiting dignitary feel at ease while aboard an American ship.

There was a funny incident that occurred during President Aleman's visit to Washington. An official dinner was organized at the Mexican Embassy in honor of President Truman. As the toasts began, a strange noise was made when everyone around the table stood up. The chairs had stuck to all of the guests like glue, except for the two leaders, whose chairs were covered with velvet. The other guests' chairs had been freshly painted, and though it had dried, it became glue-like in the heat.

☙

In August and September of 1947, I, along with my fellow stewards, served aboard the battleship *Missouri* on President Truman and his family's round trip to the International Monetary Conference held in Brazil. We stayed aboard during the conference, but I was attached to the presidential family while they were on the ship.

The president maintained his daily routine while aboard the big battleship. As usual, the boss was up early and, after a few refreshments and ice water, he started a long walk around the great man-of-war ship. Accompanied by one or two Secret Service men, he had much more walking space on the *Missouri* than on the *Williamsburg*. Back in his quarters, the president read the daily order and the news bulletin published every day aboard the battleship. When he and his guests were ready for breakfast, they went to the dining room, where I was waiting for them with the other stewards to take orders. After eating breakfast, the president took a seat in a comfortable stuffed chair and read something or chatted with his guests until everyone finished eating. Mrs. Truman and Miss Margaret eventually joined them. The boss then enjoyed another cup of coffee with his wife.

For the rest of the day aboard, President Truman spent his time reading, conferencing, or playing medicine ball or other games with his guests. When we crossed the equator, the traditional ceremony took place for those first timers, but the presidential family was exempt.

On this trip, the first lady and her daughter did not have their maids with them, so I did my best to make the voyage as comfortable as possible for them. They kindly accepted my help, but even with my years of practice and service to first families, there was one thing I could not do. I tried unsuccessfully to encourage them to let the ship's attendants take care of their personal laundry. Indeed,

53

their faithfulness to the Truman family's personal responsibilities was stronger than all my efforts of persuasion and readiness to serve.

During the return trip from South America, I heard one member of the president's party ask why he had designated the USS *Missouri* for the Japanese surrender. The second anniversary of the surrender had just been celebrated. The president answered that he had three important reasons for this. The first was that Missouri is his home state; the second reason was that the *Missouri* was the most beautiful and powerful American battleship. The third reason the president shared was that the big battlewagon had been christened by Miss Truman, his daughter.

Shortly after our return, I received a message that was sent from the president to the commander and everyone under him. It read:

> *Your Commander-in-Chief takes this means of telling all hands that he is proud of the conduct of the officers and men of Task Force 84 during the recent visit to Rio De Janeiro. Not a single discreditable incident occurred. This record of high standard of conduct brings great credit alike to our Navy and to our Nation. You have made a contribution of inestimable value to the furtherance of our Good Neighbor Policy. In fact, you have been in a real sense true ambassadors of goodwill. From my own observation I was very much impressed with your fine appearance and your department and I heard only the most complimentary remarks concerning you, so I say to all hands "Well Done."*

છ

My Filipino comrades and I were with President Truman during his historic whistle-stop campaign for the presidency in September and October 1948. As it is well known, the first lady and Miss Truman were also on the presidential train throughout the whole campaign. The boss had a relatively big staff accompanying him. We traveled from the East Coast to the West Coast, stopping at hundreds of big and small places; we covered over thirty thousand miles.

The boss gave more than three hundred and fifty speeches during this campaign. I watched as he always introduced the first lady and his daughter to the crowd; they reflected a typical American family. Mrs. Truman remained quiet even during the excitement of the campaign. The president's daughter was a dynamic campaign worker. At every stop, the president always delivered effective words to the citizens gathered around his train. I remember one speech that was especially successful. The commander in chief emphasized that he had served as a battery commanding officer on the French battlefield in World War I. I recall whenever President Truman mentioned the late FDR, the audience answered with thunderous applause.

Recalling and comparing my experiences with President Roosevelt's three campaigns, the general atmosphere was somehow different. During the time of the Great Depression and World War II, President Roosevelt was a living historical figure who represented a kind of savior in the eyes of the people. It seemed to me that President Truman was rather the historical fighter who constantly proved that he was ready to fight for a good cause up to the very end.

At the end of October, the presidential train stopped at Kansas City, where the boss gave his final fiery and valiant speech. On Election Day, I was amused by members of the press who had never left us since the first days of the campaign. They became desperate because they lost the president; they could not find him anywhere. This was a funny story. He had gone to Independence to vote and wait there for the election results, but in the afternoon, no one on the presidential train knew where the president had gone.

The mystery remained unsolved up to early the next morning, when the president appeared in Kansas City. The whole world knew that he had been elected president of the United States with a comfortable majority. We found out later that he had secretly "escaped" the news media with a few Secret Service men before the election results were final.

Something else happened on this presidential train after the clos-
ing of the campaign and on the way back to the White House. The boss
came to our kitchen compartment, shook hands with us (Filipino navy
stewards), and expressed his thanks for our good services during the
campaign. As he shook each of our hands, he placed in them a brand
new twenty-dollar bill.

∾

The president's inauguration was preceded by a memorable incident known by all the White House staff personnel and presidential
attendants. The Inaugural Committee made a mistake and sent an invitation to Mr. and Mrs. Harry S. Truman. The typical, friendly reaction from the president made me smile. The president "conditionally"
accepted the invitation, depending "on weather conditions." I admired
his good-naturedness. On the day of the event, the inaugural parade
passed, according to tradition, on Pennsylvania Avenue from the White
House to the Capitol.

∾

After the beginning of this next term, President Truman spent
some time aboard the *Williamsburg* with friends. As always, it was
my job to assist where I was needed. My colleagues and I served refreshments at these parties. The boss and his guests discussed his great
popularity in the country as it reflected in the election results. I also
observed the president graciously signing autographs and remarking
with a smile, "I think that nowadays my signature is worth at least ten
dollars." I thought immediately that, in his modesty, President Truman
underestimated the value of his autograph.

∾

In July of 1949, I served as chief steward aboard the little yacht
Margie, a presidential day cruiser that bore the name of Miss Margaret

Truman. A big party was organized aboard in honor of the vice president. I remember many senators were invited, among other guests. We stopped at the Marshall Amusement Park, near Mount Vernon.

ஒ

October 24, 1949, was an especially great day for me. I went with President Truman to New York for the ceremony of laying the cornerstone of the United Nations Building. General Carlos Romulo of the Philippines, who was the president of the General Assembly of the United Nations, was also there. The two presidents greeted each other. At the site of this historic ceremony, President Truman said, "General Romulo, you are the president of the greatest organization in the world." I recall the Filipino general replying, "Mr. President, you are the president of one of the greatest countries in the world." Hearing this exchange of historic compliments, I was so proud to be an American citizen who was born in the Philippines.

ஒ

I remember New Year's Eve 1949; the president celebrated with his assistants and guests aboard the *Williamsburg*. Once again, my fellow stewards and I assisted with refreshments, cocktails, and then dinner. Just before midnight, we prepared the champagne glasses. When the clock struck twelve, the boss and his guests held their glasses high and made toasts for the New Year of 1950. Afterward, the president left the dining room for a few minutes to call the first lady and Miss Truman on the phone. When he returned, the celebration continued. President Truman sat before the piano and played song after song as his guests sang to the music. The president retired in his stateroom and left the yacht the next morning after breakfast.

Who knew then what this year of 1950 and beyond would bring?

ஒ

During these years, I observed the commander in chief confidently working on the endless tasks of leading in war while aboard the *Williamsburg*. Our armed forces were engaged in a mortal struggle in Korea. This did not mean that anything changed in the president's kind and friendly character; he was just completely consumed in his responsibilities as commander in chief. I would serve him lunch and notify him for his meetings.

President Truman continued to spend many weekends aboard the *Williamsburg* and in the Little White House at Key West, but these were not times of rest and relaxation for the boss. The president spent all his time in conferences, meeting with national and allied leaders, studying reports, and writing documents. There were no more parties for entertaining; as time passed, the boss seemed to be confident and steadfast in his duties. It was impossible to be discouraged in his presence.

The president's one form of relaxation remained during this period: playing the piano when he was by himself. I remember when he was aboard one Saturday in November 1950; there was a conference scheduled with military and civilian advisers. I served the boss a light lunch in his stateroom, then he sat at his piano and played some music. As I listened, I was so happy to see the president detach himself from his great responsibilities, even if just for a little while. After his short rest, I signaled the boss as his advisers arrived aboard; the war meeting began.

❦

On Election Day, November 4, 1952, my fellow navy stewards and I went with President Truman, the First Lady, and Miss Margaret to Independence, Missouri, to vote. We stayed on the presidential train while the first family went to their home. On our way back to Washington, I remember that the president was calm and cheerful when he was with his family. When he joined his staff in another car, the boss became serious with the others as they anxiously awaited the voting results. Before we reached Washington, the president was informed that General Dwight Eisenhower had won the presidency. President Truman sent a message of congratulations to General Eisenhower. At Union Station in Washington, the president and first lady shook hands with all the other stewards and me; they graciously thanked us for our good services during the trip.

☙

I spent the rest of my duty in the service of President Harry S. Truman aboard the presidential yacht *Williamsburg,* anchored near the Naval Gun Factory in Washington, DC. As the date of the incoming president's inauguration approached, I wondered whether I would have the chance to say goodbye to the boss before he returned to private life. Before Christmas, I received, like all the other stewards aboard, a beautiful card from President Truman and the First Lady. A view of the White House from the East Garden was captured on the front of the card, and it was embossed with the seal of the Presidency of the United States.

I almost gave up the hope of seeing the boss again and consoled myself with the group picture I have of all the presidential attendants. I am kneeling in the front center with President Truman standing behind me. This picture had been taken one day to commemorate our services to the president, who joined us at the last minute. It was his way of showing us his great kindness. I was grateful to have this historical picture as one of my prized possessions.

I was content with this, but I did not consider the president's unparalleled thoughtfulness. On Christmas Eve of 1952, my division officer informed me that the presidential stewards would be transported by bus from the Naval Gun Factory to the White House to be received by the presidential family. You could hear and feel our great excitement! Dressed in our best gala uniforms, we took the twenty-minute bus ride to the White House. It seemed way too long for every one of us.

As soon as we reached the Executive Mansion, we were led into the south side receiving room on the first floor. We formed a semicircle, and then President Truman, the First Lady, and Miss Truman entered

In the dining room aboard the USS Williamsburg

the room. Presidential aides immediately began to present each steward to the first family. When my turn came, the president's aide stumbled when announcing my name. President Truman was the first to pronounce my name correctly and distinctly. "How do you do, Esperancilla? Merry Christmas and Happy New Year, my friend." I was extremely honored to hear my name pronounced so clearly, because this was one thing my last boss could not do. I was choked with emotion, as were the other *Williamsburg* stewards. The opportunity to say farewell to an outgoing president was given to me once again—the second one among the three I had the great honor to serve. (The late President Roosevelt made me proud many times with a handshake, but when he left this world, I did not have the chance to say goodbye.)

ை

After my service in the United States Navy ended, President Truman visited the Library of Congress, where I worked as a guard after I retired. He recognized me immediately, greeted me, and shook my hand. This brief meeting and reconnection with President Truman was recorded in the Library's *Information Bulletin* (1959):

> "... *Mr. Truman strode inside the south door*
> *to find—on duty at his regular post—Guard Iri-*

> *neo Esperancilla, old friend and once Chief Steward aboard the Presidential yacht Williamsburg. Mr. Esperancilla, who recalled he had last seen Mr. Truman on January 21, 1953, retired from the U.S. Navy in 1955 after 30 years that included service under four Presidents."*

Our picture was taken together and after receiving it, I sent a copy of the photograph to my former boss, and he graciously signed it.

HARRY S. TRUMAN
INDEPENDENCE, MISSOURI

May 14, 1959

Dear Esperancilla:

You do not know how very much I enjoyed seeing you in Washington, your birthday card and the wonderful box of candy you sent to Mrs. Truman. We both made very good use of that gift.

I hope that everything will continue to go well with you.

Sincerely yours,

Mr. I. Esperancilla
The Library of Congress
Washington, D. C.

CHAPTER 5

A Glimpse with President and Mrs. Eisenhower (1953–1955)

I had become a witness of American and world history. . . .

(I waited for my new boss; I already had the honor to know him as the victorious military leader under my two previous commanders in chief.)

While the United States transitioned presidents and administrations, there was apparently no change in sight for the presidential yacht *Williamsburg* and its personnel. After the inauguration of President Eisenhower in January of 1953, the yacht remained tied up along the dock of the Naval Gun Factory in Washington, DC. This hopeful expectation seemed even more promising when, about a month later, orders came to the skipper to move the yacht to the naval shipyard of Norfolk, Virginia, for a general overhaul. When this was completed with a trial run, we returned to the Naval Gun Factory in Washington. Indeed, the old and exciting preparations broke out again aboard the *Williamsburg* at the end of March 1953. We received orders to make the ship ready for a conference between President Eisenhower, the prime minister of France, and their advisers. On this historic occasion, I served as chief steward. The Filipino navy stewards were back at our familiar routines, doing our best to accomplish our duties. During the short cruise, we served refreshments and a light lunch to the gentlemen. We returned to Washington in the afternoon.

In May of 1953, I received word that President Eisenhower, the new First Lady, and their guests would embark for a four-day pleasure cruise. From the captain down to the youngest enlisted man, we worked hard and happily prepared the presidential cruise for the first family. We earnestly hoped that the president would enjoy himself so much that he would decide to keep the *Williamsburg* as a presidential yacht.

When the presidential party was aboard, the yacht got underway, heading to Annapolis, Maryland, and then to Norfolk, Virginia. During the whole trip, I got the impression that the distinguished guests were having a wonderful time, especially the president. He seemed quite comfortable, walking around the deck with his guests and even humming at times. A White House staff member told me he had never seen President Eisenhower so cheerful and relaxed. I was once again honored to have a part in serving a president of the United States.

After this short cruise, we returned to Washington. The presidential party left the yacht at Alexandria, Virginia, where the White House limousines awaited them. I took a few days of leave and went to my own home in DC. My devoted wife, Maryann, who was all too familiar with my presidential experiences and stories, asked me my thoughts about the ship. I told her that I was confident that the USS *Williamsburg* would continue to be part of the pages of history.

❧

As a navy seaman, when you like a ship, it is like a living being. You love it, and you cannot get accustomed to the idea that it might cease to be. The more its existence seems to be in danger, the more you hope it will escape its threatening fate. It is a great honor to be in the service of the president of the United States, but what a glorious thing it is to accomplish most of this service in the unique and unparalleled intimacy of a presidential yacht. I am expressing my own personal feelings, but I am sure the former crew, especially my Filipino comrades, would completely agree. At this point in my career, I had twenty-three years of presidential service behind me and had spent twenty-one of these years aboard presidential yachts. I hoped fervently, as all of my colleagues did, that I would finish my long tour of duty aboard the USS *Williamsburg*.

We had one last hope. We learned that our commanding officer and the naval aide to the president had made plans to redesign the presidential quarters of the *Williamsburg*. It was a question of either making a door on the wall between the bedrooms, or making one large bedroom out of two. Then, just a few days later, this hope was gone. The president announced that the USS *Williamsburg* would be decommissioned. Although I did not know the reasons behind this decision, I could not deny my feelings of personal loss.

We had a few more cruises before decommissioning. The president ordered several groups of wounded and hospitalized veterans of the Korean War to be invited aboard the *Williamsburg*. This was a great reflection of the heart of our commander in chief. He acknowledged their sacrifices. The veterans had a fine time aboard; some of them even played the piano that had once been used by President Truman. We cruised several times with them on a familiar route.

Aboard USS Williamsburg *serving wounded veterans, US Navy Photo*

With the decision to decommission, the order was given to transfer all furniture and equipment to Camp David. This was the new name given to the presidential retreat in Maryland that was formerly known as Shangri-La under Presidents Roosevelt and Truman.

℃℈

Along with my fellow comrades, as well as some new ones, I returned to my old quarters near the Blue Ridge Mountains in Maryland and slowly became accustomed to calling it Camp David instead of Shangri-La. This was my main station during my last two years of special service. During this period, I was once again honored to serve the president, who enjoyed many weekends and short getaways there with his family and friends; what a blessing this was for me.

The president's party usually consisted of a few close friends who were not connected to his work. Guests who were high officials rarely visited Camp David with this president that I can remember.

As I recall, President Eisenhower was generally up every morning around seven thirty and drank black coffee. His breakfast usually consisted of fresh fruit, minute-boiled eggs, bacon and sausage, toast and muffins, honey and marmalade, and more coffee. Every once in a while, a good-sized steak completed this substantial breakfast menu. (I am only reporting here details I recall up to July 1955.)

The president usually had his first golf party of the day around nine thirty in the morning at Camp David. The rest of the day was spent on official work, more golfing, playing bridge, and painting.

I discovered that painting was President Eisenhower's favorite hobby. I knew that he painted in the White House during his free time, but here, at Camp David, he was able to paint with fewer distractions. It was always a pleasure watching the boss busy at work painting portraits of his family members, mostly his grandchildren, and sometimes members of his Cabinet. He seldom painted living models; he used photographs and pictures, which he attached to his easel. I noticed that the drawings were made in advance, and the boss brought them to life with colors. Working on his paintings, President Eisenhower seemed content and relaxed. When he completed a portrait, he proudly showed it to Mrs. Eisenhower or his guests. The president carried his famous Ike grin when he was complimented on his work.

ᥱ᧒

As a general observation of the boss at Camp David, his social habits reminded me of President Hoover at Camp Rapidan. President Eisenhower had a small circle of personal friends at the camp.

The boss liked to eat outdoors with his family and guests, weather permitting, so every step was taken to ensure a pleasant experience for all. A general rule at these parties seemed to be that one guest always brought an extra aged wine, brandy, bourbon, or scotch.

The highlight of the Camp David dinners was when President Eisenhower himself became the cook. By four thirty in the afternoon, the boss was already in our kitchen to direct and supervise the preparation of the tenderloin steak (which he would broil outside for his guests). He gave instructions to the chef to soak the meat in lots of melted butter and garlic salt. About forty-five minutes before dinner, it was my job to prepare and heat the charcoal on the outdoor grill. Then the president would come, tying a steward's apron around his waist, and place the meat on the grill. The boss would watch with the eyes of a real chef for a few seconds. He would tend to the steak, moving back and forth from the guests to the grill. The president also prepared the tasty sauce for the meat. The look on his face captured the joy he felt when the guests complimented him, asking for more of his famous tenderloin. I often thought photographers should be present to capture these proud and priceless moments of President Eisenhower cooking.

I am a professional cook and have watched many of my great colleagues in the kitchen. In my opinion, President Eisenhower seemed to be a real master of the culinary art when he was behind the outdoor grill.

ᥱ᧒

I had the good fortune of closely observing the moving relationship between President Eisenhower and his little grandson, David. He was the miniature image of his grandfather. He was a typical child, very friendly with everyone he met and full of questions. It was a pleasure to watch him with his grandfather; the young boy followed the president everywhere he could. They played golf together, and little David did not take his eyes off his grandfather, even when President Eisenhower was engaged in conversation with other adults.

The famous photograph of President Eisenhower on the golf course with his grandson sometime in 1953 is a great illustration of their profound attachment to each other. The picture shows the president bowing and shaking hands with little David, who is also bowing to his grandfather. In my opinion, this is the best picture ever taken of the famous granddaddy and his equally famous grandson.

When the president was painting and his grandson was around, David always stood behind him and admiringly watched the paintbrush in movement. Sometimes the little boy sat as a model for the presidential artist; at these times I think that both of their faces were worth painting by another artist. Whenever they were together, they were alike in so many ways.

∽

The launching of the USS *Nautilus* took place with Mrs. Eisenhower in January of 1954. The other stewards and I were invited to witness this event; what an honor that was! We had to take a train to get there, and we were given assistance from the Secret Service men and the electric boat ushers to return.

∽

In August of 1954, a Cabinet meeting was held at Camp David. After the meeting, a buffet dinner was offered outside of the "Big House," which was the new name of the presidential quarters (the late President Roosevelt called it "Bear's Den"). I assisted the presidential

THE WHITE HOUSE

WASHINGTON

20 January 1954

MEMORANDUM FOR:

Chief Esperancilla

You and the other stewards are invited to witness the launching from Bleachers B. You need the enclosed blue card to get in.

You are to get lunch on the train for yourselves, Rose Wood and Mitchell.

It is important that you get back to the train immediately after the launching. Chief Langello, the Secret Service men, and the Electric Boat ushers have been alerted to help you get back. It is important that you do not delay because the train has to pull out at 11:10 a.m.

EDWARD L. BEACH
Commander, U. S. Navy

Memo to attend the launch of USS Nautilus

couple and the members of the Cabinet as chief steward.

Everyone was in good spirits, including the Secretary of Defense. The first lady was the center of the distinguished company. While dessert was served, I passed around the president's guest book for everyone to sign. I had selected Good Humor ice cream for dessert; the boss really liked it and even asked for a second helping. As he enjoyed dessert, I saw a glimpse of his grandson and namesake.

ↄ

Mrs. Eisenhower reminded me of the late Mrs. Hoover. She always accompanied her husband on weekends and vacations; her main task was to help the president get a good rest. Like Mrs. Hoover, Mrs. Eisenhower watched and ensured that nothing would disturb the president unnecessarily. When he went fishing or to play golf, the first lady stayed at home and waited patiently for his return. I especially remember how devoted Mrs. Eisenhower was to the president. I often observed her calming demeanor when at Camp David.

❦

I also witnessed the endearing relationship between President Eisenhower and his mother-in-law, Mrs. Doud. She was a very likeable lady, and at family dinners, she always sat to the right of the president, who listened with interest and respect to everything she said. The boss called her "Min" and always seemed ready to give her a helping hand if needed.

❦

One of my responsibilities in the service of our presidents was to see that the guest book was signed by every guest visiting the chief executive wherever he was (when I was on duty). At Camp David, no important visitor escaped my vigilant request to sign the guest book. One day, I had the idea of asking the Eisenhower grandchildren to sign the book. There were no great difficulties with the older children, David and Barbara, signing the book, but with little Susan, the kind first lady offered to help. The youngest grandchild at the time called her presidential grandparents by their famous nicknames, Ike and Mamie. Mrs. Eisenhower guided Susan's little hand as she wrote her very first signature of her young life. This operation took quite some time, so I remember telling Mrs. Eisenhower, "Maybe Miss Susan will be a first lady, and she would be happy to see her first signature." The first lady replied, with a wink and a big smile, "We can never tell, can we?"

❦

All the stewards in the presidential household were Filipinos. We all became proud Americans; however, we never forgot our beautiful native islands. Everything that reminded us of our homeland was music to our hearts. Earlier I described the late President Roosevelt naming our quarters in Shangri-La "Little Luzon," after the largest Philippine archipelago. My comrades and I were so touched, and that name, "Little Luzon" brought us true joy every time we stayed there.

One day at Camp David, Mrs. Eisenhower gave us a gift that brought that same joy to our hearts. She came to the camp for the weekend with President Eisenhower, and the first lady presented us with a basket full of fresh mangoes, a favorite fruit of every Filipino. What gave her this thoughtful idea? I immediately remembered that at the beginning of the president's military career, he spent some years in the Philippines with General Douglas MacArthur. Mrs. Eisenhower was there with him and experienced the terrible heat of summer in the Philippines. She also learned from our native population to love the tropical fruits during her time there. It was hot that weekend when the first lady gave us the touching gift of mangoes, and we were profoundly grateful for her thoughtfulness.

❦

Most of my service to President Eisenhower was at Camp David, but there were a few times I was ordered, with other stewards in my charge, to go to Washington to serve the president and his guests at intimate luncheons and dinners. These meals usually took place in a room just across from the president's office.

In spite of my short stays at the Executive Mansion, I was able to observe the president's typical days in the White House. He worked hard throughout the day, and his work ended with dinner while I was in the White House. I also observed that President Eisenhower enjoyed playing bridge, both in the White House and on vacation at Camp David.

❦

In early 1955, President Eisenhower and the First Lady invited the White House staff to a party at the Eisenhower farm in Gettysburg, Pennsylvania. At that time, I was the chief of naval stewards in the service of the president. My fellow stewards and I were called from Camp

David to serve at Gettysburg for this occasion. We prepared the tables in the spacious garden of the mansion. The party went very smoothly, and I observed President Eisenhower and the First Lady being charming hosts. We returned to Camp David late in the evening.

❧

The time arrived for my long-planned retirement from the United States Navy. My request had been approved, and my retirement date was set for July 15, 1955. As July 15 drew closer, by the order of the naval aide to the president, this date was postponed due to one final assignment. I was greatly honored to receive the official orders—to serve President Eisenhower at the Summit Conference in Geneva, Switzerland.

I went to Geneva ahead of the presidential party with a group of Secret Service men, White House staffers, and stewards. We took off at the Military Air Transport Service section of Washington National Airport in July of 1955, and we landed at the beautiful Geneva-Cointrin Airport the next day. We were sent ahead to organize the presidential mess. This included the quarters for personnel, food, refreshments, silverware, chinaware, glassware, linens, and any other essential equipment and supplies needed during the presidential party's stay in Switzerland. The secretary of state, other Cabinet members, and other prominent figures were in this presidential party.

Geneva was one of the most beautiful cities I had ever seen. It surrounds the tip of the famous Lake of Geneva at the point where the Rhone River begins its course toward France. The city appears to be both modern and ancient, existing in the shadow of great mountains. In good weather, walking on the flowered boardwalk, I could see the majestic, snow-covered Mont Blanc. This is Europe's highest mountain.

The presidential party stayed at the Chateau du Creux de Genthod, a few miles from the city on a lakeside slope. To me it looked almost like our White House, both the inside and outside. The grounds were very well kept; the rose garden was full of blooming roses of the most beautiful colors. I also remember tall, artistically trimmed evergreen plants. They looked like strange pagodas from a distance. There was a boathouse a short distance from the villa near the lake, and we filled it with the best selection of international liquors. A member of the presidential party reminded me immediately after his arrival to make sure we had a good supply of Russian drinks and authentic vodka for the expected guests.

The president and Mrs. Eisenhower brought their son with them on this trip. It was my impression that the first family was satisfied with the work done in the villa before their arrival. They enjoyed the American food that we served. From their first day there, Mrs. Eisenhower actively presided over the temporary Geneva household. Along with her secretary, I went every morning to see the first lady to discuss the menu for the day.

I recall an especially successful menu one day when President Eisenhower, the First Lady, and a few staff members ate lunch at the villa. I honestly do not remember everything I served for that meal, except for the vegetables. I served corn on the cob and okra. The boss enjoyed it with a good appetite, and he turned toward me when he finished. With his famous grin, he said, "Somebody around here knows what I like to eat. Corn with okra is my favorite dish." I truly appreciated the president's acknowledgment of our selections and service.

The long line of callers for the president was headed by the foreign chiefs of government. I had the pleasure to see and serve Sir Winston Churchill again. I am sure that he recognized me when I approached him with a glass of whiskey on my tray. He took it and thanked me with a gracious smile. As I looked at him, I think we both recalled so many historic moments in the presence of the late President Roosevelt and President Truman. I also served the French premier, whom I had never seen before nor since.

I thought the most interesting guests were the Russian guests. In my experience with Soviet leaders, I found the Russian premier to be a fine and cultured gentleman. I recall that Mr. Khrushchev was boisterous and friendly, while another Russian (military) leader kept a smile on his face.

We left Geneva on July 24, and we were back in Washington the next day. My final special assignment was over.

ເຈ

On my very last day in the United States Navy at Camp David, I assisted President Eisenhower, the First Lady, and their guests as usual. This presidential party began with morning golf. While they played, I retrieved the golf balls, handed towels to the gentlemen, and served refreshments while they were resting. After golf, I served at the cocktail party that followed in the enclosed porch of the Big House. A bridge party began as I continued my last day of duties. I remember clearly the president looked at me and said, "What is this bad news I hear? Are you leaving us, Chief?"

With all the guests now listening, I replied, "Mister President, I am retiring now because I would like to get another job before I am fifty years old." President Eisenhower then asked me how much my retirement pay would be, and we had quite a meaningful exchange of ideas and thoughts about the retirement conditions for service members and the strict limitation of their earnings while receiving a pension from the government. Then the boss gave me a warm handshake, followed by his guests, and I left the room. This conversation with President Eisenhower was profound to me. I felt that he was genuinely concerned and understood the challenges of a man in the military like me.

ເຈ

Before I left Camp David and the grandiose scene of American history, I had a pleasant surprise. My commanding officer told me to go outside on the lawn for a picture with all my colleagues. This would be a treasured souvenir of my quarter-century tour of duty in the service of our last four presidents. As the photographer arranged our group, President and Mrs. Eisenhower joined us and took seats in the middle. I was honored to be seated near President Eisenhower and the First Lady. This is one of many pictures I cherish as a reminder of my service to our country. My military service to this president ended in July of 1955. I was confident that with prayer and honest leadership, we would enjoy peace and prosperity for many years under President Eisenhower.

Chief Esperancilla seated second to the left of President Eisenhower

CHAPTER 6

A Glimpse of Retirement and Beyond

I wondered often at the miracle of God which was my destiny. . . .

Since the summer of 1955, I have been out of the glare of history that has shone around me for a quarter of a century. As I grasp this new life season, I often look back and reflect.

The following words are from a memo written to me by my officer in charge:

For the benefit of those who have not observed the efficient and capable method in which ESPERANCILLA accomplishes all duties assigned to him, it must be emphasized that his soft-spoken, unpretentious manner belies his high capacity for leadership. . . .

I received this final memo in 1955 from the naval aide to the president of the United States:

I shall depart from the official form of correspondence in this instance inasmuch as I feel this should be made instead a personal statement of my own high regard for you.

You will retire from the Navy in July of this year after thirty years of active service. I cannot but feel the deep sense of loss to this office, to the Navy and to all of us aware of your faithful and almost legendary service to Presidents Hoover, Roosevelt, Truman and finally President Eisenhower. When all the histories for this era are written you may indeed have the gratification of reading between the lines and knowing to what extent you played an important part in the making of these histories. During the famed trips of the former Presidents, and in helping them fulfill engagements with the distinguished guests they have entertained and were entertained by in the United States and in other countries—your knowledge, understanding, leadership ability and the necessary tact and courtesy required, which you never failed to exhibit, contributed much to the ease and success of all the functions involved. There was never concern as to the successful outcome of any services rendered by you. Your assured manner and unvarying competence left nothing to be desired. For all this you have a right to feel singularly rich in memories of a job well done.

Your service record, while officially correct as to your outstanding service, does not give you full justice for the many unwritten talents contributed by you to each instance of your assigned missions. Were detailed credits to be written I'm sure they would fill many pages. It is understandably not possible to list them all. . . .

I am deeply grateful for these kind words, but I am less sure about my personal role in making history during my service to four presidents of the United States. I know that I did not have any part in history during these twenty-five years. I was in the rare position in the history of our country of observing closely these four leaders of the greatest democracy in the world, not only as living and legendary historical figures but also as human beings.

I was honored to receive a commendation from President Eisenhower after my retirement. He wrote a letter to the secretary of defense, reflecting his heartfelt thanks to those who served him. I was reminded of that final conversation with a president; my observations and belief in his honest leadership reflected in his words and actions.

❧

I still wear a uniform, which is that of a special guard's unit in a federal administration building (Library of Congress) in Washington, DC. I am very happy in my present modest job because I have something to remember. Occasionally, I have the great pleasure to see again, either at official ceremonies or in the newspapers, former Presidents Hoover, Truman, and Eisenhower. I can no longer see the boss whom I served for the longest time, during the most beautiful years of my own life, the late President Roosevelt. I now have a hope which warms my heart. . . .

There will soon be a marble statue of FDR along the Potomac, between the Jefferson and Lincoln Memorials. Thus, there will be a place for me to immerse myself in the glorious past, while watching the rapid flow of the Potomac and the inexorable passing of the time.

CHAPTER 7

A Glimpse of IE's
Words and Pictures

*It was given to me to see with my eyes the prodigious
March of Time—a great, maybe the greatest, change
in the course of American history.*

The great opportunity when one serves a president is to simultaneously see the maker of history *and* the human being.

Human beings never know today what the next day will bring to them.

I can summarize all my experiences in one sentence: He who reaches the presidency of the United States is not only a great human being, but also a great gentleman.

Card signed by President Hoover

Chief Esperancilla standing to the right of FDR aboard USS Houston *with crew*

Parade cover signed by President Truman

Signed photo from President Eisenhower

Final Thoughts—A Glimpse from a Granddaughter

I did this job, which was the dream of my young years as a Filipino high school boy. . . .

I marvel at this "job" of being a presidential steward in the US Navy during my grandfather's time in service. From looking through every note, menu, and order that was given, I have just a glimpse of the great responsibilities and burdens the stewards carried on a daily basis while they served. With each day that passed, I'm sure the glory of serving a president was also overshadowed by that longing for family, for loved ones, for home, but still these navy stewards persevered and served quietly behind the scenes.

In addition to the tasks my grandfather described, the role of chief steward also involved shopping for the proper quantities of food needed for events and creating itemized lists of food purchases while keeping costs to a minimum. My grandfather kept written records and hand-typed pages of these items. While planning menus and serving, stewards had to remember certain items that could not be served, as well as items to serve to particular guests exclusively, such as certain cocktails offered to French officials (dry vermouth with a twist of lemon peel and crushed ice).

Chief stewards ensured that everything was in order for presidential parties, meals, and daily living to run smoothly. From preparing and inspecting linens in the bedrooms to properly placing silverware and chinaware in the dining rooms, all the Filipino stewards worked diligently behind the scenes. These stewards left a lasting impression on all they served; I have found letter upon letter conveying the deep appreciation and high regard for their outstanding service.

1. ~~Sherry~~
2. ~~White~~ Wine – Fish
3. ~~Burgundy~~ – meat
4. ~~Champagne~~
5. ~~Liqueurs~~ *Wines*

J. Esperancilla
19 JUNE 1951

United States Naval Station
Key West, Florida

Dinner

(3) CHAMBERTIN 1947 *serve third*

(1) AMONTILLADO – *serve first*

(2) SCHLOSS VOLLARDS 1947 *serve second*

(4) CHARLES HEIDSIECK 1943 *serve fourth*

(5) LIQUEURS *serve last*

HORS D'OEUVRES
CHILLED VICHYSOISSE
CELERY HEARTS   OLIVES   RADISHES   PICKLES
BAKED RED SNAPPER
PARSLIED NEW POTATOES
FILET MIGNON
MUSHROOMS GARNISHED
BRAISED CELERY   ASPARAGUS
LEMON BUTTER SAUCE
PARKERHOUSE ROLLS   ASSORTED JELLIES
ENDIVE SALAD
ROQUEFORT CHEESE   OIL DRESSING
CRACKERS
VANILLA ICE CREAM
BRANDIED CHERRY SAUCE
COFFEE   NORRIS MINTS   CHOCOLATES

Menu with Chief Esperancilla's notes

1935

U.S.S. HOUSTON

BREAKFAST

Grapes	Figs
Oranges	Prunes
Grapefruit	Apples
Honeydew Melon	Cantaloupe

Other Fruits in Season

Corn Flakes	All-Bran
Post Toasties	Puffed Wheat
Shredded Wheat	Grapenut Flakes

Grape Nuts

Oatmeal	Wheatena

Cream of Wheat

Eggs to Order

Bacon	Sausages
Shad Roe	Finnan Haddie
Mackerel Roe	Yarmouth Bloater
Kippered Herring	Mackerel (Salted)

Fresh Fish as Caught

Waffles	Hot Cakes

Sirup   Honey

Toast	Hot Muffins
Strawberry Preserves	Orange Marmalade
Coffee	Tea

Fresh Milk   Cocoa

One of Chief Esperancilla's many typed presidential menus

U. S. S. MISSOURI
NAVAL DISPATCH

10 September, 1947

FROM: THE PRESIDENT

TO: The Commander Task Force 84.

Please transmit the following to the Force under your command.   Quote   Your Commander-in-Chief takes this means of telling all hands that he is proud of the conduct of the officers and men of Task Force 84 during the recent visit to Rio de Janeiro.   Not a single discreditable incident occurred.   This record of high standard of conduct brings great credit alike to our Navy and to our Nation.   You have made a contribution of inestimable value to the furtherance of our Good Neighbor Policy.   In fact, you have been in a real sense true ambassadors of good will. From my own observation I was very much impressed with your fine appearance and your deportment and I heard only the most complimentary remarks concerning you, so I say to all hands "Well Done"   unquote.

Harry S. Truman

Letter from President Truman following trip to Rio de Janeiro

U.S. NAVAL ADMINISTRATIVE UNIT
POTOMAC RIVER NAVAL COMMAND
U. S. NAVAL GUN FACTORY
WASHINGTON 25, D. C.

21 June 1955

TO WHOM IT MAY CONCERN

1. Upon his retirement in July 1955, Irineo ESPERANCILLA, SDC, USN
will be completing a long and distinguished career with the U.S. Navy.
During his career, ESPERANCILLA has served Presidents Hoover, Roosevelt,
Truman and Eisenhower. For more than ten years he has been in charge of
all the Navy Stewards rendering service to the First Family. His service
record is filled with letters of appreciation for services performed for
the above presidents, their families, and their many important guests
from every part of the world.

2. For the benefit of those who have not observed the efficient and
capable method in which ESPERANCILLA accomplishes all duties assigned to
him, it must be emphasized that his soft-spoken, unpretentious manner
belies his high capacity for leadership and comprehension. His record
of service, with its many indications of the satisfaction and pleasure
of all persons whom he has served, is in itself sufficient indication of
ESPERANCILLA's capabilities.

3. ESPERANCILLA's retirement will be a great loss to the Navy and
particularly to this unit in which he has served so well. There is no
doubt, however, of his ability to succeed in whatever field of civilian
endeavor he may choose. He carries with him the very best wishes and
heartiest recommendation of every officer and man with whom he has served.

WALTER C. SLYE
Lieutenant Commander, U.S. Naval Reserve
Officer-in-Charge

Letter from Lieutenant Commander upon Chief Esperancilla's retirement

❦

In addition to his remarkable life as a chief steward in the US Navy, Irineo was also a devoted husband, father, and grandfather. During his time in Washington, he met and married Maryann Pettie. She had one son, Lorenzo, my Uncle "Buzzy," who later had four children.

My grandmother affectionately called my grandfather "Renny." Together they had one daughter, my mom, Ann, who was born in 1940. Serving her whole life as a navy family member, she married a navy recruit from the Philippines (Johnny Paje) in 1966; my parents had four children.

My grandfather began writing his memoirs with the vision to publish a book describing his experiences as a presidential steward. His story was featured in *Look* magazine, as well as on an NBC news show. Understandably, life continued, and years went by; the book was a vision not yet realized.

My grandfather was diagnosed with colon cancer in the 1970s and made one last trip to the Philippines to see his family. This remarkable man passed away in July of 1976, about four months after his youngest grandchild, my brother, Joey, was born.

I was only three years old in 1976, but I can clearly remember the times that I took short trips in the car with my grandfather when he took my older brother and sister to school. He would take me to my grandparents' house afterward, where he made me cream of wheat. Little did I know the hands that prepared and served my breakfast had also prepared and served state dinners and meals for former presidents of the United States, as well as world leaders like Sir Winston Churchill.

My beautiful grandmother proudly displayed the picture of my grandfather that appears on the front cover in her home. She was *his* glimpse of greatness on the home front, always praying for his safe return. She kept my grandfather's legacy alive, telling stories of his life, sharing souvenirs and keepsakes of his time in service, and taking our family to Arlington National Cemetery, where he was buried. My brothers, sister, and I, along with our children, still visit my grandfather's grave to this day.

After the loss of my grandparents and then my own parents, it was hard to believe that *A Glimpse of Greatness* would ever become a reality; in the words of my amazing grandfather, "It was a miracle of God which was my destiny." I am grateful for this opportunity to be the voice for my grandfather's story. Putting the parts of this book together has given me greater insight and appreciation for who I am and where I came from. Although there were several newspaper articles written about his experiences, none can compare to my grandfather's original thoughts and perspective as he lived during those extraordinary times.

Through my grandfather's words, I see the magnificence of the US Navy ships during times of war and times of peace. I hear the laughter and the tension of figures in history, both well known and unknown. Most of all, I feel the longing of those Filipino stewards, who faithfully served a country that was not their first home. As I read the letters and memos that were written to my grandfather so long ago, I am in awe of the lives he touched and influenced, simply by putting forth his very best at the job he was given.

It is my hope that this glimpse into the journey that my grandfather and other brave Filipinos took so many years ago has opened your eyes to the quiet greatness that is often necessary to change lives, perspectives, and even the course of history. May you find in your own family's stories a glimpse of greatness. . . .

References

Bureau of Naval Personnel. "Filipinos in the United States Navy."
   Naval History and Heritage Command, 2017. https://www.
   history.navy.mil/research/library/online-reading-room/ti-
   tle-list-alphabetically/f/filipinos-in-the-united-states-navy.
   html.
Rigdon, William. *White House Sailor.* Garden City: Doubleday,
   1962.